# *Thomas Alva Edison*

## THE MAN WHO
## ILLUMINATED THE WORLD

*Thomas Alva Edison*

# THE MAN WHO ILLUMINATED THE WORLD

A PICTORIAL BIOGRAPHY

by
Lawrence A. Frost

AMEREON HOUSE
MATTITUCK

Ron Ziel photo

Dedicated to Norman R. Speiden
who has devoted 34 years to the
preservation of the Edison story.

International Standard Book Number 0-8488-1718-4 *hardcover*
International Standard Book Number 0-8488-1719-2 *softcover*

*To order contact*
AMEREON HOUSE,
*the publishing division of*
Amereon Ltd.
Post Office Box 1200
Mattituck, New York  11952-9500

*Proudly manufactured in the United States of America*

# Foreword

Thomas Alva Edison was destined to change the ways of the world. It was not his plan to do so; it was his fate. Early in life he displayed a nature and personality different than that of his playmates.

Inquisitive, sensitive, imaginative and industrious from childhood on, he constantly sought answers to the numerous questions that perplexed his active mind.

His schoolteachers didn't appreciate his constant flow of questions; his father thought him stupid. But his mother always understood him. She was his mentor. Her influence, her appreciation of and faith in him guided him through life.

Refusing to attend school after learning that his schoolmaster had considered him "addled," his mother conducted a daily schedule of reading, writing and arithmetic.

He was uninterested in the outdoor activities of other children, preferring to remain indoors and read. Because of this he developed an interest in experimentation.

By the time he was twelve he had obtained a job selling newspapers and acting as a candy butcher on the Grand Trunk Railway's run between Port Huron and Detroit.

With the advantage of a remarkable memory he had the incredible ability of separating the right from the wrong answers in an unbelievable variety of interests. This stood him in good stead in later years when conducting his countless experiments.

Patience was his principal virtue. Rarely did he center his interest on one thing at a time. His active, inquisitive mind was quickly and easily, though temporarily, diverted from any experiment that revealed a phenomenon or reaction he could not understand. His reaction was one of pursuit. And pursue it he did. Offtimes the discovery led to another invention.

It was his practice to read everything obtainable on a subject then direct his approach to its solution along an unprecedented route.

Of a restless nature he constantly searched for better ideas and solutions to the many questions that plagued his inquisitive mind. Neither time nor expense hindered his efforts. In one instance, almost 50,000 experiments in five years were conducted in his search for an alkaline storage battery to propel his electric automobile. His associate, after 9,000 such experiments on it, remarked that it was a shame there had been no results. Edison smiled and replied, "Results! Why man, I have gotten a lot of results! I know several thousand things that won't work."

He was suspicious of formal education in the realization he had been unhampered by one. He had been permitted to select his own subject matter for study. An unusual background and unregimented schooling appear to be instrumental in such a reaction.

Like fellow Ohioan General George Armstrong Custer he didn't believe in crying over spilt milk. He said he had spilt a lot of it but quickly forgot it when he did. There was everything to be gained by keeping the pathway of his creative thought processes clear.

From the time he first boarded a train in Port Huron he displayed an interest in travel. Once he had learned enough to operate a telegraph key in Mount Clemens, Michigan, he obtained employment as a telegraph operator in Sarnia, Ontario. From there he moved to Adrian, Michigan; Toledo, Ohio; Fort Wayne, Indiana; Cincinnati, Ohio; Louisville, Kentucky; Nashville and then Memphis, Tennessee; Boston, and finally to New York. From that point on he made inventing his business.

Though best known for his invention of a practical incandescent light many are unaware that it became the cornerstone of a new industry. From it stemmed the electric generator, electric motor, electric train and electric automobile, and the General Electric Company, to name a few.

The incandescent lamp literally illuminated the civilized world. It turned night into day. And although Alexander Graham Bell is credited with inventing the telephone it was Edison's improvements to the telephone that made it practical for all purposes.

Success did not curb his imaginative powers for next came the phonograph, the motion picture camera and projector, and numerous other inventions in many unrelated fields. From 1869 to 1910 he applied for 1,328 separate patents.

The "Wizard of Menlo Park" as he was known, became mankind's greatest benefactor. Henry Ford considered him to be our greatest American, an opinion no one can dispute. Certainly no American in his day created more employment or made a greater impact on industry, business and home life. The results of his busy brain has touched, influenced and affected almost everyone in the civilized world from that day until this. Perhaps no person has done more to benefit mankind. Truly, Thomas Alva Edison was the king of creativity.

LAWRENCE A. FROST
MARCH, 1984

# Acknowledgements

Each of my previous album subjects have been controversial personages, each being of a military figure whose rise to fame was based on merit, ability and temperament. The subject of this album was as unmilitary a figure as this nation could produce yet one whose contributions did more for the nation's future than the military actions of the others.

By chance a highway sign on the Ohio toll road drew me into Milan, the "Birthplace of Edison." A delightful, informative tour through Thomas Alva Edison's birthplace residence, conducted by Laurence Russell, its curator, awakened an interest in this great American. Encouraged by Mr. Russell, a visit to the West Orange Laboratories in New Jersey — a national historic site maintained by the National Park Service — became mandatory.

The kindly attention of Norman R. Speiden, Supervisory Museum Curator of the West Orange Laboratories, encouraged me further, and to the extent that a number of return trips were arranged. Mr. Speiden has read every word of this volume and called my attention to a number of errors. Should any now be evident he should be relieved of all blame for I accept the sole responsibility of the final draft.

The Honorable Charles Edison, former Governor of New Jersey, and the son of Thomas Alva Edison, has evidenced his deep interest by reading this manuscript and making a number of suggestions that improved and made the final draft more accurate. Any evident inaccuracies are not of his making.

Kathleen L. McGuirk, Archivist of the Edison National Historic Site, presides over 11,000 negatives and vast amounts of Edison correspondence and records. She spent days on end "bending over backwards" in providing material, arranging for prints, answering letters, and making useful suggestions.

Mrs. Madeleine Edison Sloane, president of the Edison Birthplace Association, gave encouragement.

Mrs. Bertha Emmons, Chief Librarian, and Mrs. Melba A. Mitchell, hostess of the Milan Museum; Mrs. John Sharpe, assistant curator at the Edison Birthplace Museum, and Wallace White, Milan historian, gave me considerable assistance.

James G. Cook, Executive Director of the Thomas Alva Edison Foundation; R. C. Halgrim, curator of the Thomas Alva Edison Home at Fort Myers, Florida; Robert V. Spelleri, Publicity Director of the Western Union; Miss Jean Sonnhalter, Public Relations Department of the Firestone Tire & Rubber Company; R. L. Howsam, Jr., International Press Relations Department of the General Electric Company; Jeannette E. Range, Librarian of the Consolidated Edison Company of New York, Inc.; Monica J. Maier, Librarian of the Detroit Edison Company; Lewis S. Gum, Historian of the American Telephone and Telegraph Company; Lois B. Thompson, Chief Librarian, Stratford (Ontario) Public Library; Mrs. Eva Jane Dunn, Local History Librarian, St. Clair County Library; Elliott N. Sivowitch, Division of Electricity and William E. Geoghegan, Division of Transportation, Smithsonian Institution; John Heath, Ranger Historian and Paul B. Kasakove, Ranger and former associate of Edison, Edison National Historic Site, contributed unselfishly of their time and knowledge.

The staff of the Monroe County Library and particularly of the Dorsch Memorial Library rendered invaluable service in obtaining elusive Edison material.

John S. Manion, Syracuse, New York, provided valued assistance.

Roy Hamlin made many useful suggestions that substantially improved the text and interest.

I would be remiss if I did not express my gratitude to Superintendent Roy W. Weaver, Edison National Historic Site, W. Don Horn, of West Orange, New Jersey, and Jed Clauss, chairman of Amereon Ltd., for their deep interest and efforts toward revising and reprinting this book.

Especial thanks to John C. F. Coakley, Historian of the Edison Pioneers, who compiled the Chronology of the events in the life of Thomas Alva Edison.

To my secretary, Mrs. Harriet Jennette, and my wife, Ethel, my thanks for typing and proof-reading the entire manuscript.

L. A. F.


Monroe, Michigan
April, 1969
October, 1983

# Table of Contents

"He has led no armies into battle. He has conquered no countries. He had enslaved no peoples. Yet he wields a power the magnitude of which no warrior has ever dreamed."

Arthur J. Palmer
October 21, 1931

"To find a man who has not benefitted by Edison and who is not in debt to him, it would be necessary to go deep into the jungle. I hold him to be our greatest American."

Henry Ford

"I have been asked what a man over 70 can do to keep occupied. The trouble is, that a man who can't keep busy didn't take interest in a great number of things when he was mentally active in his younger years . . . . There are a great many hobbies he can work with and keep busy until his death."

Thomas Alva Edison

# A CHRONOLOGY OF
## EVENTS IN THE LIFE OF
# THOMAS ALVA EDISON
### 1847 — 1931

Samuel Insull stated, "I never attempted to systematize Edison's business life. Edison's whole method of work would upset the system of any office. He would just as likely be at work in his laboratory at midnight as midday. He cared not for the hours of the day or the days of the week. If he was exhausted he might more likely be asleep in the middle of the day than in the middle of the night, as most of his work in the way of inventions was done at night . . ." 1889. Edison National Historic Site.

1847 February 11—born at Milan, Ohio, son of Samuel and Nancy Elliott Edison.

1854 Edison family moved to Port Huron, Michigan.

1857 Earliest record of interest in chemistry—young Tom Edison had a laboratory in the cellar of Port Huron home.

1859 A newsboy and "candy butcher" on the train of the Grand Trunk Railway, running between Port Huron and Detroit.

1862 Printed and published a newspaper, "The Weekly Herald," on the train—the first newspaper ever printed on a moving train.

1862 August—saved from death the young son of J. U. MacKenzie, Station Agent at Mt. Clemens, Michigan. In gratitude, the father taught Edison telegraphy.

1862-3 During this winter, Edison used a locomotive whistle to telegraph across the river between Port Huron, Michigan, and Sarnia, Ontario, when a telegraph cable broke due to an ice jam.

1863 Put up a telegraph line from Port Huron railway station to the village and worked in the local office.

1863 May—first position as regular telegraph operator on Grand Trunk Railway at Statford Junction, Ontario, Canada.

1863 Began a five-year period during which he served as a telegraph operator in various cities of the Central Western States, always studying and experimenting to improve apparatus.

1868 Made his first patented invention—the Electrical Vote Recorder. Application for patent signed October 13, 1868.

1869 Landed in New York City, poor and in debt. Shortly afterwards, looking for work, was in operating room of the Gold Indicator Company when its apparatus broke down. No one but Edison could fix it and he was given a job as superintendent.

1869 October — established a partnership with Franklin L. Pope as electrical engineers. This partnership, although of brief duration, resulted in the invention of the "Universal" Stock Ticker, also the "Unison" device for automatically bringing into synchronization all stock tickers on a given circuit.

1870 Received his first money for an invention—$40,000 paid him by the Gold and Stock Telegraph Company for his stock ticker. Opened a manufacturing shop in Newark where he made stock tickers and telegraph instruments.

1871 April 9—death of mother, Nancy Elliott Edison. She was born January 4, 1810, the daughter of the Rev. John Elliott.

1871 December 25—married Mary Stilwell, daughter of Nicholas Stilwell, of Newark, New Jersey.

1872 Began a four-year period during which he conducted manufacturing of telegraph instruments for Western Union Telegraph Company and Automatic Telegraph Company. He had several shops during this time in Newark, New Jersey. He worked on and completed many inventions, including the motograph, automatic telegraph system, duplex, quadruplex, and multiplex telegraph systems; also paraffin paper and the carbon rheostat.

1873 April 23—sailed for London on the S. S. Java, called the "Jumping Java." This was Edison's first trip abroad. He demonstrated the use of his automatic telegraph over long circuits and submarine cables. He returned to Newark, June 25, the same year.

1875 November 22—discovered a previously unknown and unique electrical phenomenon which he called "etheric force." Twelve years later this phenomenon was recognized as being due to electric waves in free space. This discovery is the foundation of wireless telegraphy.

1876 March 7—applied for patent on his invention of the "electric pen." Patent was granted August 8, same year. Licenses covering the pen were later obtained by the A. B. Dick Company of Chicago, for the manufacture of the mimeograph.

1876 April—moved from Newark to his newly constructed laboratory at Menlo Park, New Jersey. This was the first laboratory for organized industrial research.

1877 April 27—applied for patent on the carbon telephone transmitter which made telephony commercially practicable. This invention included the microphone which is used in radio broadcasting.

1877    December 6—recorded "Mary Had a Little Lamb" on the tinfoil phonograph. This was the first time a machine had recorded and reproduced sound.

1877    December 24—applied for U. S. Patent on the phonograph.

1878    February 19 — phonograph patent granted without a single reference. U. S. Patent No. 200,521.

1878    April 18—took the tin-foil photograph to Washington, D. C., to demonstrate it before the National Academy of Sciences and to President Rutherford B. Hayes and White House guests.

1878    May-June—in an article in the "North American Review" he foretold ten important uses for the phonograph.

1878    July 29—using the heat of the sun's corona during an eclipse at Rawlins, Wyoming, he tested the microtasimeter, a device for indicating minute heat variations by electrical means.

1878    September 8—accompanied by Professor George F. Barker and Professor Charles F. Chandler, he visited William Wallace in Ansonia, Connecticut, where he became actively interested in the problem of electric lighting.

1878    October 15—incorporation meeting of the Edison Electrical Light Company.

1879    July—first Edison experimental marine electrical plant installed aboard S. S. *Jeannette* for the George Washington De Long expedition to the Arctic.

1879    Invented the first practical incandescent electric lamp. The invention was perfected October 21, 1879, when the first lamp embodying the principles of the modern incandescent lamp had maintained its incandescence for more than forty hours.

1879    Invented radical improvements in construction of dynamos, making them suitable for generators for his system of distribution of current for light, heat and power. Invented systems of distribution, regulation and measurement of electric current, including sockets, switches, fuses, etc.

1879    December 31—gave a public demonstration of his electric lighting system in streets and buildings at Menlo Park, New Jersey.

1880    Discovered a previously unknown phenomenon. He found that an independent wire or plate, placed between the legs of the filament of an incandescent lamp, acted as a valve to control the flow of current. This became known as the "Edison Effect." This discovery covers the fundamental principle on which rests the modern science of electronics.

1880    April 3—invented the magnetic ore separator.

1880    May 1—first commercial installation of the Edison lighting system on land or water was installed on the S. S. *Columbia.*

1880    May 13—started operation of the first passenger electric railway in this country at Menlo Park, New Jersey.

1880    Ushered in seven strenuous years of invention and endeavor in extending and improving the electric light, heat and power systems. During these years he took out more than 300 patents. Of 1,093 patents issued to Thomas A. Edison, 356 deal with electric lighting and power distribution.

1880    October 1—first commercial manufacture of incandescent lamps began at Edison Lamp Works, Menlo Park, New Jersey.

1881    January 31 — opened offices of the Edison Electric Light Company at 65 Fifth Avenue, New York City.

1881    March 2—Edison arranged to open the Edison Marchine Works at 104 Goerck Street, New York City, in a building formerly used by the famous old shipbuilder, John Roach, for his Aetna Iron Works.

1882    January 12—opened the first commercial incandescent lighting and power station at Holborn Viaduct, London, England.

1882    May 1—moved the first commercial incandescent lamp factory from Menlo Park to Harrison, New Jersey. Organized and established shops for the manufacture of dynamos, underground conductors, sockets, switches, fixtures, meters, etc.

1882 September 4—commenced the operation of the first commercial central station for incandescent lighting in this country at 257 Pearl Street, New York City.

1883 July 4—first three-wire system central station for electric lighting started operation at Sunbury, Pennsylvania.

1883 November 15—filed patent on an electrical indicator using the Edison Effect. This was the first patent in the art of electronics.

1884 August 9—his wife, Mary Stilwell Edison, died at Menlo Park, New Jersey.

1885 March 27—patent executed on a system for communicating by means of wireless induction telegraphy between moving trains and railway stations.

1885 May 14—patent executed on a ship-to-shore wireless telegraphy system, by induction.

1886 January—bought Glenmont,. a residence in Llewellyn Park, West Orange, New Jersey.

1886 February 24—married Mina Miller, daughter of Lewis Miller, founder of Chautauqua, inventor and manufacturer of agricultural machinery, of Akron, Ohio.

1886 December — moved plant of Edison Machine Works from 104 Goerck Street, New York City, to Schenectady, New York.

1887 November 24—moved his laboratory to West Orange. During the first four years of his occupancy of his West Orange laboratory, he took out over eighty patents on improvements on the cylinder phonograph. He established a very extensive business in the manufacture and sale of phonographs and records, including dictating machines, shaveable records and shaving machines.

1889 October 6—first projection of an experimental motion picture. This was a "talkie" shown at the West Orange laboratory; the picture was accompanied by synchronized sound from a phonograph record.

1891 August 24—applied for patent on the motion picture camera. By the invention of this mechanism, with a continuous tape-like film, it became possible to take and reproduce motion pictures as we have them today.

1891 This year marked the culmination of his preliminary surveys and experimental work on iron ore concentration which he had started while in Menlo Park in 1880. Edison did some of his most brilliant engineering work in connection with this project. Actual work was commenced in his great iron ore concentrating plant at Edison, New Jersey, during 1891 and this enterprise was continued till 1900.

1893 Edison-Lalande primary cells supplied power for the first electric semaphore signal installed on a railroad near Phillipsburg, New Jersey.

1894 April 14—first commercial showing of motion pictures took place with the opening of a "peephole" Kinetoscope parlor at 1155 Broadway, New York City.

1896 Experimented with the Xray discovered by Roentgen in 1895. Developed the fluoroscope which invention Mr. Edison did not patent, choosing to leave it to public domain because of its universal need in medicine and surgery.

1896 February 26 — death of his father, Samuel Edison, in Norwalk, Ohio.

1896 April 23—first commercial projection of motion pictures at Koster & Bial's Music Hall, New York City, by the Edison Vitascope.

1896 May 16—applied for a patent on the first fluorescent electric lamp. This invention sprang directly from his work on the fluoroscope.

1900 This year marked the beginning of a ten-year period of work which resulted in the invention of the Edison nickel - iron - alkaline storage battery and its commercial introduction. The alkaline battery is widely employed as a power source in mine haulage, inter and intra plant transportation, for railway train car lighting and air conditioning, signalling services and many other industrial applications.

1901 Commenced construction on the Edison cement plant at New Village, New

Jersey, and started quarrying operations at nearby Oxford. In his cement industry, Edison proceeded to apply the fruits of experience gained in the iron ore concentrating venture.

1902 Worked on improving the Edison copper oxide primary battery.

1903 July 20—applied for patent on long rotary kilns for cement production.

1907 Developed the universal electric motor for operating dictating machines on either alternating or direct current.

1910 This year initiated a four-year period of work on an improved type of disc phonograph. His work resulted in production of the "Diamond Disc" instrument and records, which reproduced vocal and instrumental music with improved fidelity.

1913 Introduced the Kinetophone for talking motion pictures, after spending much time on its development.

1914 October 13—patent executed on electric safety lanterns which are used by miners for working lights. These miners' lamps have contributed in an important degree to the reduction of mine fatalities.

1914 Developed a process for the manufacture of synthetic carbolic acid. Designed a plant, and within a month was producing a ton a day to help overcome the acute shortage due to the World War.

1914 December 9—Edison's great plant at West Orange, New Jersey, was destroyed by fire. Immediate plans for rebuilding were laid and new buildings began to rise almost before the ruins of the old were cold.

1914 Invented the Telescribe, combining the telephone and the dictating phonograph, thus permitting the recording of both sides of telephone messages.

1915 Established plants for the manufacture of fundamental coal tar derivatives vital to many industries previously dependent on foreign sources. These coal tar products were needed later for the production of wartime explosives. Mr. Edison's work in this field is recognized as having paved the way for the important development of the coal tar chemical industry in the United States today.

1915 October 7—became President of the Naval Consulting Board, at the request of Josephus Daniels, then Secretary of the Navy. During the war years, he did a large amount of work connected with national defense, particularly with reference to special experiments on over forty major war problems for the United States Government.

1923 Made a study of economic conditions, the result of which was published in a pamphlet in 1924, when Mr. Edison presented to the Secretary of the Treasury a proposed amendment to the Federal Reserve Banking System.

1927 Began a four-year period during which Edison was searching for a domestic source of natural rubber. After beginning the serious study of botany at the age of 80, he collected and tested in his chemical laboratory over 17,000 different plants. Some rubber was found in about 1,200 plants and commercial quantities in 40 species. Goldenrod *(Solidago leavenworthii)* was chosen because it would grow anywhere in this country, was a one-season crop, the reaping of which could be done by machinery. This project was completed by the vulcanization of goldenrod rubber shortly before his death.

1928 October 20—received a special Congressional Medal which was presented by Andrew W. Mellon, Secretary of the Treasury.

1929 October 21—commemorating the Fiftieth Anniversary of the incandescent lamp and in the presence of President Hoover, Henry Ford and other world leaders, Mr. Edison re-enacted the making of the first practical incandescent lamp.

1931 October 18—died at Llewellyn Park, West Orange, New Jersey, at the age of 84; survived by his wife, Mina Miller Edison, his four sons, Thomas Alva, Jr., William Leslie, Charles and Theodore, and his daughters Marion Edison Oser and Madeleine Edison Sloane.

Compiled by John C. F. Coakley, Historian of Edison Pioneers.

Revision of 1969

Chapter One

# Haven In Ohio

Dr. Leman Galpin administered a few hearty slaps to the buttocks of a newborn baby. It was early in the morning of February 11, 1847. The baby's cry of indignation announced to the neighbors that Sam Edison had another mouth to feed.

Sam's wife, Nancy had a difficult delivery. In her seventh pregnancy she was middle-aged, and the child had an unusually large head, so the doctor thought. Now it was over and time for Sam to get the medicine Dr. Galpin requested.

After briefly stopping at the neighbors to give them the tidings he ran the few blocks to the village square and its only pharmacy. The night previous a heavy snow had blanketed the hogback on which he lived but it offered little resistance to his long, powerful legs.

Milan, Ohio, had been good to him. He had lived there almost nine years. It had been his haven in time of need for he had left Canada with the law on his coat tails. Here his shingle mill had provided him with a comfortable though not luxurious livelihood. Though his wants were simple he visualized a great future for himself.

Milan, to him, was a town with a future and he intended to grow with it. A shingle mill today could be a lumber mill tomorrow. He was in on the ground floor of opportunity and intended to make the best of it.

George Lockwood and Ebenezer Merry had a vision. Milan was on the Huron River eight miles south of Lake Erie. Why not build a tow path from the mouth of the river to Abbotsford? A canal could be dug the remaining three miles to Milan so that lake schooners could be towed all the way.

The Milan Canal Company was incorporated in 1827 for $35,000 with stock at $50 a share and $20,000 in bonds sold additionally. Construction began in 1833. The Huron River was shunted through Merry's old mill race — a course it follows today—and the old river bed was dug out to form a basin. The three-mile-long canal leading to the basin, containing two locks, was 40 feet wide and 13 feet deep.

The Milan Canal Basin at the time was 600 feet long, 250 feet wide and 15 feet deep. Thirteen warehouses lined the south side and in the banner year of 1847 they handled 917,800 bushels of wheat and over a million bushels of corn. On a single day in 1847, it is recorded, a six-mile lineup of 600 wagons unloaded 35,000 bushels of wheat. Hogs, cattle, lumber, barrel staves, potash, whiskey and wines were cargo items too.

In 1824, when the canal construction was in the talking stage, the village of Milan had a population of 675. With the completion of the canal in 1839, the benefits were immediate. Tolls realized in the first five years amounted

to $102,000, resulting in stockholder dividends of $20,000.

With the shipping and shipbuilding, the port trade amounted to several million dollars a year. With this boon the sleepy village suddenly stirred out of its slumber. An influx of rough living seamen, shipyard hands and towpath teamsters kept the three taverns and uncounted grog shops in a state of activity and turmoil. Brawls and gang fights were common occurrences amongst the water front workmen. It was to this "Odessa" of America that Sam Edison had come to build a new life.

Samuel Edison, Jr., had been a native of Canada. Of part English, part Dutch ancestry, he had unbounded energy, ambition, stamina and determination. He was born on August 16, 1804, in Nova Scotia, the sixth of eight children to Samuel Edison, Sr., and Nancy Stimpson Edison.

The first Edison to reach this continent was a widow Edison who had landed at Elizabethport, New Jersey, about 1730, from the Netherlands. Bringing with her an only son John, three years of age, she never remarried.

John Edison, having inherited a valuable estate, married Sarah Ogden on October 10, 1765, settling upon a farm in the Passaic valley of Essex County, New Jersey. His loyalty to the King became evident during the Revolution. When the Whigs took over Essex County on October 20, 1776, John with his family and some other Tories took refuge in New York within the British lines. When Washington's army was forced southward, John enlisted with General Howe as a scout against Continental guerrillas in the New Jersey hills.

On February 27, 1777, he and his brother-in-law Isaac Ogden were captured and imprisoned for more than a year in the Morristown jail. Had he taken the oath of allegiance to the Continental Congress he would have been freed. But he refused.

Tried for high treason before the New Jersey Council of Safety in January, 1778, he was convicted and sentenced to be hanged. Members of his and the Ogden family who had served with the Continental Army used their influence in his and Isaac Ogden's behalf and had their sentences commuted. They were paroled later that year.

With the confiscation of all their property following the Revolution, the Edisons sailed from New York on September 23, 1783, as emigrants. In return for their property loss the British Government awarded them some land on the bleak east coast of the Bay of Fundy in Nova Scotia. It was there in 1804 that Samuel Edison, Jr., the father of Thomas A. Edison, was born.

Canada was calling for settlers. After 28 fruitless years in Nova Scotia, the Edisons accepted 600 acres of timber along the Otter River in Ontario, two miles from Lake Ontario. They made their move in the spring of 1811.

They were settled less than a year when the Empire was at war with the United States. Sam Edison, Sr., like his father John, was loyal to Great Britain. After raising a company of volunteers, he served as a captain of the First Middlesex Regiment under Colonel Thomas Talbot. Late in 1814 he retired from service, returning to his Ontario homestead.

Around 1820 the settlement became known as the village of Vienna. It was here that Sam Jr. met Nancy Elliott, a teacher of a two-room school and the daughter of a Baptist minister, the Reverend John Elliott. They were married in Vienna, Ontario, September 12, 1828.

Sam Jr., like all of the Edisons, was an individualist. He had tried his hand at carpentry and tailoring, and finally settled on innkeeping. Though his education was slight—he could barely write enough to make out bills for his father—he took a great interest in governmental affairs.

Four children were born to Sam and Nancy in Vienna: Marion in 1829; William Pitt in 1832; Harriet Ann in 1833; and Carlile in 1836.

After taking part in an unsuccessful move to overthrow the Royal Canadian Government in 1837 under the leadership of William Lyon MacKenzie—the issue was home rule—Sam had to run to safety. The long legs of his powerful six foot one-inch body enabled him to run 80 miles in two and a half days to the frozen St. Clair River, crossing it to a haven at Port Huron, Michigan.

Now safe in the very country his father had fought against in the War of 1812, he made plans for a future in exile. A new frontier was opening in the midwest; the region offering opportunities that appealed to an opportunist like Sam was Milan, Ohio. He arrived there alone in 1838.

Sam's first efforts were put into the construction of a shingle mill. With some financial help from his family and encouragement from Captain Alva Bradley, he was able to set up

NANCY ELLIOTT EDISON, the mother of Thomas Alva Edison, was the daughter of Baptist Minister John Elliott. She married innkeeper Sam Edison Jr. in 1828, in Vienna, Ontario. Courtesy Edison National Historic Site.

SAMUEL EDISON Jr. was hotheaded and stubborn like his father. Involved in a rebellion against the Royal Canadian Government, he was forced to find refuge in Michigan. Edison National Historic Site.

17

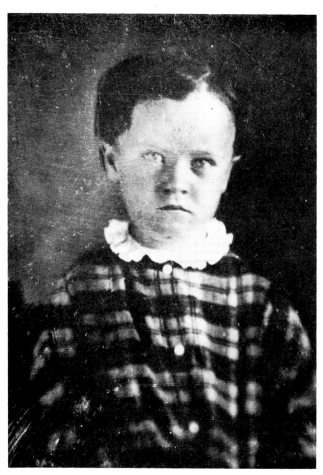

**THOMAS ALVA EDISON AT FOUR YEARS OF AGE.** Though a sickly child, he always mustered up enough energy to get into some kind of scrape. Ca. 1851. Edison National Historic Site.

"While a newsboy on the railroad I got very much interested in electricity, probably from visiting telegraph offices with a chum who had similar tastes to mine." 1857. Courtesy Edison National Historic Site.

**EDISON'S BIRTHPLACE.** This Milan, Ohio, house occupies a ridge overlooking the Milan Canal Basin. Maintained by the Edison Birthplace Association, it is open to visitors. One block away is the Milan Historical Museum, former residence of Dr. Lehman Galpin, the physician who attended Mrs. Edison at Tom's birth. Ca. 1889. Edison National Historic Site.

**WHEELING AND LAKE ERIE RAILROAD,** sometimes called the "Wheelbarrow & Leg Weary Railroad," bordered the Milan Canal Basin. An old canning factory is in the foreground. Ca. 1878. Milan Public Library.

When calling at Luther Burbank's California home Edison was asked to sign the guest book. Under "Occupation" he wrote, "Interested in Everything." Emil P. Spahn photo. 1880. Edison National Historic Site.

his new enterprise in less than a year. Then Captain Bradley shipped Canadian lumber to him to be made into shingles. With the business under way by the spring of 1839, Bradley ferried the Edison family across Lake Erie from Canada on one of his barges.

Sam selected an acre of land overlooking the Milan Canal Basin, paying $220 for it. With his own hands he built a frame and brick house facing the Hogback Road — presently called Choate Lane — the seven-room structure being completed in 1841.

Sam bolstered his income during the early years by aiding in the construction of the Plank Road, now known as Route 601. Some of his pay was received in bonds the last of which he cashed in December, 1847.

His wife Nancy attended the Milan Presbyterian Church regularly, taking their daughter Marion with her. Sam was just too busy. His brother Thomas had acquired a sloop on which they transported cedar logs for the shingle mill. Sunday was just another day on which to work.

It was at the Milan Presbyterian Church the seventh baby was baptized Thomas Alva; Thomas after his father's brother, and Alva after Captain Alva Bradley, his father's best friend.

Sam had discovered that one could get into trouble in church. While his father was a member of the Baptist Church in Port Burwell, Canada, both his father and mother had been voted out of it for ridiculing it and refusing to obey its rules. Sam, Jr., concluded that the shingle mill was a place where he could speak as he wished on Sunday.

Edison's faculty for delegating details was enhanced by having a stenographer at his elbow and a bookkeeper nearby to record the results. He said, "I have tried a million schemes that will not work. I know everything that is no good. I work by elimination." Photo by S. A. Holmes, May 4, 1878. Courtesy Edison National Historic Site.

"Mr. Edison is the most widely informed man I have ever come in contact with; not only in his scientific knowledge, but also his general knowledge is well-nigh universal," said Harvey Firestone. Ca. 1880-1881. Edison National Historic Site.

Henry Ford stated that, "He (Edison) does not like formality and will seldom attend public dinners or anything of the kind . . . He is an inexhaustable man of funny stories and he could occupy a whole afternoon, starting in at China and giving examples of story-telling in every race and nation and dialect." Hanns Hanfstaengl photo, Berlin. 1881. Courtesy Smithsonian Institution.

"My desire," said Edison, "is to do everything within my power to further free the people from drudgery, and create the largest possible measures of happiness and prosperity." Anderson photo, New York City, June 25, 1881. Edison National Historic Site.

The Canal Basin was extremely busy those days. It had become a Great Lakes port, its 13 warehouses a scene of extensive activity. On some days as many as 20 schooners could be seen in the area. A shipbuilding industry had laid ways on which some 75 vessels would be built.

The kitchen door of their new home faced a slope that spanned the several hundred feet down to the canal basin, the hogback on which the house was built being about 85 feet above the canal. With the family shingle mill at the foot of the slope and grain elevators, a tannery, a flour mill, a brewery and several blacksmith shops fringing the edge of the basin along with the warehouses, little Alva was exposed to a scene he would never forget.

In later years when reminiscing with Henry Ford he recalled that in 1850 or 1851, six covered wagons camped in front of his home while preparing for a trek to the California gold fields. During the gold rush to California, Milan too felt the impelling urge to go West.

It was about this same time he discovered a bees' nest. While he was in the act of digging it out a ram attacked him, butting him severely. Though hurt and badly shaken he managed to climb a nearby fence to safety, aborting the animal's preparation for another attack.

He recalled that at the age of five he was "driven by a carriage from Milan, Ohio, to a railroad, then to a port on Lake Erie, thence by a canal boat in a tow of several to Port Burwell in Canada, across a lake, and from there we drove to Vienna, a short distance away." He remembered his grandfather Edison sitting under a tree in the middle of the day constantly chewing tobacco while he nodded his heavy head of white hair at passing friends. As he moved toward the house with the aid of a very large cane, he resisted the offers of assistance.

Alva viewed his grandfather as a personage, and since it was always at a distance he never experienced the pleasure of a child on a grandfather's knee. He remembered seeing Dutch appurtenances around the house such as a trunk, a molasses jug and various pipes.

No more mischievous than others his age, he was certainly more curious. This curiosity led him toward the grain elevators and the flour mill. On an expedition to the grain elevator he fell into the pit and would have been smothered by the grain spilling into it had he

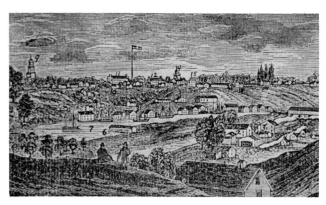

**MILAN, OHIO, IN 1846.** View from the Sandusky City Road: 1. Townsend's old distillery in right foreground; 2. Merry's oil, saw and flour mills; 3. Choate's carding mill; 4. mill race; 5. covered bridge; 6. loading dock; 7. Canal Basin; 8. W. Choate's house to extreme left with Edison birthplace behind tree nearby; 9. Presbyterian Church; 10. John Smith's tannery; 11. Hamilton store; 12. Andrews Building; 13. Mansion House (a tavern); 14. Methodist Church; 15. Fowler's Exchange Inn; 16. Fowler's Exchange Inn barn; 17. McMillan-Standish Wagon Works; 18. Fowler residence; 19. distillery. Sketch by Henry Howe, 1846. Milan Public Library.

not been seen and quickly rescued. It was inevitable, living on the edge of a canal, that he fall into it one or more times, and on one such occasion he almost drowned.

Sam Winchester, the miller, operated his flour mill with steam. Fascinated by the noise and activity there, Alva was frequently seen with his nose pressed against the back window of the shop. Repeated warnings and spankings were useless. His mother's birth switch was not spared but had little effect. He was fascinated with watching "The Mad Miller of Milan" construct a passenger balloon, one in which the miller would lose his life. One of his flour mills had burned to the ground from the hydrogen he had used to inflate a balloon. When Alva was nearly six, Winchester made a successful ascension that carried him out over Lake Erie. His body was never recovered.

**MILAN PRESBYTERIAN CHURCH** where Thomas Alva Edison was baptized. 1857. Milan Public Library.

**SOUTH SIDE OF MILAN SQUARE IN 1847.** The telegraph office was over Ashley's Jewelry Store, the low, two-story frame building in the center. Milan Public Library.

"The Wizard of Menlo Park," so he was constantly referred to by the press. Myron Thomas photo, Shamokin, Penn. 1883. Courtesy Edison National Historic Site.

**NORTH SIDE OF MILAN SQUARE AS IT APPEARED IN 1847.** Each General Store had its backroom whiskey keg with a handy tin cup that provided a free thirst quencher before the trading began. Milan Public Library.

About this same time Alva became involved in a tragedy that occurred in a creek nearby. While he was swimming there with a playmate of the same age, the other boy disappeared under the water. Alva waited quite some time for him to reappear. When it began growing dark, Alva went on home but said nothing to his parents. During the night he was awakened and questioned. The body of the boy, a son of the proprietor of Milan's largest store, had been pulled out of the creek.

On another occasion, Alva had become extremely interested in the process of hatching eggs. After exhausting Sam and Nancy with his questions regarding the process, he disappeared for most of an afternoon. Recognizing the boy's capacity for seeking and finding trouble, his family searched his usual play areas but couldn't find him. The search ended when his father discovered him in a barn sitting on a nest he had made and then filled with goose and chicken eggs. He had hoped to hatch them.

When six years old, Alva became the recipient of a public whipping administered by his father in the Milan village square. Alva, experimentally, had built a small fire inside his father's barn on the slope in back of the house several days before. Unfortunately the barn burned down. His father made him a public example by administering a bottom warming where all could see and hear.

Alva appears to have been a perplexing problem for which Sam was unable to find a solution. The boy's active, inquisitive mind led him into places and predicaments a less vigorous mentality would not have considered. His great curiosity, his continuous flow of questions caused many people, including his father, to think the boy was of low mentality. It appears that in those days a boy who asked countless questions was considered stupid. Apparently his father — a frequent target of the constant flow of puzzling questions — maintained a similar opinion of him. Perhaps this opinion was firmed when, following his father's frequent "I don't know," the boy began countering with "Why don't you know?"

No great love developed between the father and the son. Though he maintained a certain loyalty for his father, he held a deep affection for his mother. Years later Edison said, "My father thought I was stupid, and I almost decided I must be a dunce." Unable to cope with

his problem child, Sam had reached either a point of exhaustion from the many questions hurled at him, or he did not know the answers —probably both.

To a writer on the staff of the New York *World* Edison said of his mother:

"I did not have my mother very long but in that length of time she cast over me an influence which has lasted all of my life. The good effects of her early training I can never lose. If it had not been for her appreciation and her faith in me at a critical time in my experience, I should very likely never have become an inventor . . . . She believed that many of the boys who turned out badly by the time they grew to manhood would have become valuable citizens if they had been handled in the right way when they were young.

"I was always a careless boy, and with a mother of different caliber I should have probably turned out badly. But her firmness, her sweetness, her goodness, were potent powers to keep me in the right path. I remember I used never to be able to get along at school. I don't know what it was, but I was always at the foot of the class. I used to feel that the teachers never sympathized with me and that my father though I was stupid, and at last I almost decided that I must really be a dunce. My mother was always kind, always sympathetic, and she never misunderstood or misjudged me. But I was afraid to tell her all my difficulties at school for fear she too might lose her confidence in me."

Milan's prosperity had developed a feeling of community independence for in 1853 a lake shore line called the Columbus, Sandusky & Hocking Railroad bypassed Milan by running its line to Toledo through Norwalk. The Milan villagers who owned the canal refused an offer of a railroad station and stock in exchange for a free right-of-way. Ultimately the canal traffic used the rail facilities. Milan's population dwindled to less than half, Sam Edison's business shrinking with it. Deciding that another waterfront location would be more desirable, Sam made several trips to Port Huron, Michigan, to inspect houses and potential business sites.

The move there was made in the spring of 1854. Traveling by train to Detroit, they took the paddle steamer *Ruby* across Lake St. Clair and up the St. Clair River to Port Huron.

# Chapter Two

# Seeking A New Home

Sam knew a good thing when he saw it coming. A town of 4,000 people just had to grow as a result of what was to come. Situated at the entrance to Lake Huron and just across the St. Clair River from Sarnia, Ontario, Port Huron had been selected by the Grand Trunk Railroad as the terminus of a new rail line to be extended northward from Detroit. The Canadians were building a line down to Sarnia to reach a ferryboat service across the St. Clair River that would connect the two railroads.

The Edisons now occupied the former residence of an army quartermaster. The large, solidly built, two-story colonial house stood in a grove of pine trees on the northern edge of Port Huron opposite the Fort Gratiot parade grounds. The fort once had been a French trading post but was an American army base at this time.

The six-bedroom house, surrounded by ten acres of land, offered a splendid view of Lake Huron to the north and the course of the St. Clair River to the south.

Since Sam was renting this house he had more capital to invest in his new grain, feed and lumber business. In seeking new ways to add to his income he decided that an observation tower 100 feet high with a telescope at its top would be worth 25 cents to tourists eager to see a breathtaking view of surrounding water and shore lines.

That first summer he collected three dollars though later the new railroad brought many visitors. One regular though free patron—Alva —spent a great deal of time on the topmost platform using the old telescope to scan the waterway with its constantly changing panorama of steamships, sparred sailing ships and smaller vessels.

The sightseeing novelty soon wore off and in time the neglected and unused "Tower of Babel" fell to the ground. Meanwhile Sam became involved in other business enterprises equally unproductive.

Alva first attended school in the fall of 1855. It was a one-room school conducted by the Reverend G. B. Engle. A frequent recipient of his teacher's leather strap, Alva soon found himself at the foot of the class. Three months later he overheard his instructor tell the school inspector that he was "addled" and not worthy of being kept in school. Overwrought to the point of tears, he told his mother. She took him back to school and gave the teacher a verbal shaking. At the lowest point in his young life he had discovered that his mother was, as he said, "the most enthusiastic champion a boy ever had, and I determined right then that I would be worthy of her and show her that her confidence was not misplaced."

OPPOSITE—"Putting off a thing until tomorrow was a practice unknown to Edison. He kept going forward relentlessly and when an obstacle came in his path either passed around it or turned it to his advantage," said Francis Jehl. Ca. 1847. Courtesy Edison National Historic Site.

**THOMAS AND HARRIET ANN EDISON.** Harriet Ann—the family called her Tannie—was born in Vienna in 1833. She was the fourth of the seven Edison children to die quite young. Ca. 1854. Edison National Historic Site.

There is no evidence that Alva's school problems were due to deafness, but rather to inattentiveness. His hearing, which later was impaired, was normal early in life. While receiving only three months of grammar school education, that had been delayed because he had become quite ill from scarlet fever, his wilful nature and disinterest in the formal teaching methods of that time received little sympathy from the teacher. His father thought him stupid.

Alva refused to return to school. It was then that Nancy Elliott Edison became the boy's teacher. Following her housework each morning she gave Alva lessons in reading, writing and arithmetic. More important, she taught him the purpose for, and love of, learning.

Alva was punctual at the daily classes his mother conducted and was very attentive and serious. His playmates felt sorry for him during vacation time. Yet he never complained or hesitated when his mother called.

The neighborhood children loved Mrs. Edison and she loved them. Meeting them at the gate as they passed to school, she would hand them fresh doughnuts, apples and other sweets.

A family acquaintance recalled how much alike Al and his mother were. The son's features and characteristics were like his mother's. He had the same strong chin, broad brow and deep-set eyes—and a slight smile about the lips.

Alva had the advantage of a remarkable memory. When he read anything he retained it, and he evidenced a high degree of imagination. Nancy encouraged the use of his imagination and permitted him to follow certain natural interests he had in his reading.

By the time he was nine he had read Hume's "History of England," Gibbon's "Rome" and Sear's "History of the World." About this same time he read his first book of science — Richard Green Parker's "Natural and Experimental Philosophy." About the age of ten he began trying out almost every one of the experiments in this book on elementary physics. He took nothing for granted for he wanted to find out "Why?"

A favorite retreat of his was the cellar. There it was quiet and there was ample room on the shelves for his supply of bottles and jars. He had no great desire to play outside with other boys for he had discovered a world of his own. His father misunderstood him as evidenced in a statement of his years later: "He spent the greater part of his time in the cellar. He did not share to any extent the sports of the neighborhood. He never knew a real boyhood like other boys." Sam Edison, an athletic outdoor type, just could not realize that Thomas Alva derived much more pleasure inside.

At the age of 11, Alva and the Edisons' chore boy Michael Oates prepared a large truck garden of corn, cabbages, lettuce, onions and peas. House-to-house sales in a rented horse and wagon netted several hundred dollars from that summer of "hoeing corn in a hot sun," and cured him of any interest in a future of farming.

Alva was fascinated with the engines used by the Grand Trunk Railway. The Grand Trunk leased engines from the Chicago, Burlington & Quincy Railroad. They had highly polished brass bands and painted woodwork that made them most attractive to Alva. With the opening of their Port Huron machine shops in 1859 Al spent considerable time there.

Frequently he was permitted to ride in the cab with the engineer, and occasionally he would be allowed to handle the controls. On one trip, the engineer and the fireman, who had been out all night dancing, became so sleepy they had Al run the locomotive of the slow freight while they slept. Alva reduced the speed to 12 miles an hour, bringing the seven cars safely to their destination. Along the way he became concerned about the amount of water in the boiler for he knew if it got low there could be an explosion. About 20 miles out, damp, black mud blew out of the stack, covering the engine and young Edison. This stopped, however, before he could awaken the fireman. Stopping at a station where the fireman always opened the oilcup on the steam chest near the cow-catcher to fill it, Alva proceeded to do the same. The steam rushed out with such force he was nearly knocked off the engine. With great difficulty he closed the oil cup, then got his train on the way. Later he learned that the engineer always shut off the steam before the fireman oiled the locomotive.

Another eruption of black mud occurred just before reaching his destination. When he arrived, the entire engine was covered with black mud and was the subject of considerable laughter. Edison discovered that he had carried so much water it passed over into the stack and was being blown out with the soot that accumulated there.

Disliking the task of hoeing corn in the hot Port Huron sun, and learning there was need for a newsboy on the daily train, he plagued his mother persistently for permission to apply for the job. His mother acceded to his request after he convinced her he was always short of the money needed for chemicals; selling newspapers would be a means of supplying his needs.

The Edisons were not doing as well in Port Huron as they had in Milan. Sam Edison saw no reason why Al—as his friends were calling him by this time—couldn't sell newspapers if he would be permitted to. It would take some pressure off him so he applied for, and obtained, the job for the boy.

The train left Port Huron each day at 7 A.M., arriving in Detroit at 10 A.M. While in Detroit he would buy candy, fruits and papers for sale on the train, usually spending the balance of his day at the reading room of the Young Men's Association. The train returned at 4:30 P.M., arriving at Port Huron at 7:30 P.M., Al taking his role of "candy butcher" on the way.

His industry and business sense were soon evident. After several months he had opened two stores in Port Huron; one for butter, berries and vegetables, and the other for periodicals. After placing a boy in charge of each he soon found that the one in charge of periodicals could not be trusted so he closed that store. The other was kept open for most of a year.

Transporting two large baskets of vegetables from the Detroit market each day, he would take them to his store where they were quickly sold. Purchasing butter from farmers along the rail line, and blackberries when in season—all wholesale—he sold them at a discount to the wives of the engineers and trainmen. Soon he had a boy selling bread, tobacco and stick candy to the coach loads of immigrants moving to the West.

Trains in those days were made up of a baggage car, a smoking car, a ladies' car and three coaches. One car was divided into three compartments; one carried mail, another baggage, and the third express. This latter, always unused, Al was later to fill with chemicals, telegraph equipment and his printing press. He never was asked to pay freight for the vegetables he carried in the mail car and never knew the reason why unless it was because he was small and industrious.

**THOMAS EDISON AT THE AGE OF 14.** As a newsboy and candy butcher on the Grand Trunk Railway between Port Huron and Detroit, he displayed an interest in telegraphy. 1861. Edison National Historic Site.

Earnings on the train were good, often as much as eight or ten dollars a day—out of which he would give his mother a dollar each day.

Some of the boys who worked for him—for many tried to get Saturday work with Al as candy butchers—related how quiet and preoccupied he was. He spent little time talking as he was extremely busy.

He never blackened his boots and seldom combed his hair. When the cheap suits he wore demanded replacement, the new ones were of similar low quality.

Money seemed of little interest. Any profit derived was used for purchasing more chemicals. Money was the means by which he could conduct experiments. At this point his aim in life was to become a chemist.

Al took little interest in the talk boys commonly engaged in; he spent his time studying. When not reading a book—he always carried one in his pocket—he appeared to be deep in thought. But his honesty and integrity made a deep impression upon all of his associates.

One afternoon his train jumped the track, causing four old cars to go to pieces. Figs, dates, raisins and candy were distributed all over the tracks. Not wishing to see any of them go to waste, Al ate his fill to a point his family doctor had to give him considerable attention.

He was called one evening to the office of E. B. Ward & Co., a steamship firm in Port Huron, where he was requested to carry a message of great importance. One of their steamship captains had died quite suddenly and there was need for an immediate replacement to navigate his idle ship. The retired ship captain they hoped to reach, but could not, lived 14 miles from Ridgway, Michigan, his nearest railroad station.

Offered 15 dollars, but demanding and getting 25 dollars, to deliver the message, Al invited another youngster to share the money and the trip. The two started from Port Huron at 8:30 P.M. in absolute darkness and a heavy rain. After traveling awhile their lanterns went out, and the trail they traversed over the partially cleared land become rougher than ever. Overcome by fatigue and deciding they were lost, they leaned against a tree and cried.

Extremely fatigued and scared, Al compelled himself to move on, soon reaching a highway. The 14 miles of corduroy road ahead of them was easier than the 14 miles they had traveled. There were no obstacles to stumble over, no ghostly figures of brush and trees close to them to stir their fertile imagination. Day was breaking as they knocked on the door of the captain's house. It was the most horrible night Tom Edison ever spent.

**THE LOCOMOTIVE EDISON DROVE.** While a newsboy on the Grand Trunk Railway Edison drove this engine so the fireman and engineer could catch up on their sleep. Edison National Historic Site.

**PORT HURON HAD A BUSY PORT.** Side-wheeler ferries, tugs and three-masted schooners found plenty of business on the St. Clair and Black Rivers when Edison lived there. Ca. 1860. Courtesy St. Clair County Library.

Early in the Civil War a regiment of volunteer infantry was stationed at Fort Gratiot. Since the military reservation extended to the Edison property line the night calls of the sentry were heard quite clearly. The call "Corporal of the Guard Number One" would be repeated by each sentry along the line until it reached the barracks. That corporal would move forward to see why he was being called.

One dark night Al and his Dutch playmate Michael Oates, on returning from selling papers, called out for the Corporal of the Guard Number One. This was repeated and relayed down the line of sentries, bringing the corporal up the line a half mile only to find it was a ruse. Al and his friend repeated their performance successfully a second night. On the third night the sentries were ready. They caught the Dutch lad, taking him to the barracks jail. The speedier Al headed for his home with the soldiers in close pursuit. Rushing into the dark cellar, he headed for the potato barrels. The one nearly empty was quickly emptied into the other two, then pulled over his head bottom up to rest on the floor. His father, awakened by the soldiers, aided them in their search for him. With the aid of candles and lanterns they searched everywhere. Finally they left somewhat perplexed for the corporal was certain he had seen Al enter the cellar. There was no other means of exit.

Stiffened from his cramped quarters and half sick from the evil smell of rotten potatoes that had been in the barrel, Al went to bed. The next morning he was awakened by his father who vigorously applied a switch to his bare legs. Al said this was the only occasion his father ever used a switch on him. Not so his mother for the switch she used on him had the bark worn off because of the frequency with which he had mussed up the house in the past. The Dutch lad fared the better of the two for he was released from the barracks guard house that morning unswitched.

On another occasion the Oates boy did not fare as well as his playmate. Al had been impressed with the Milan miller's attempts to inflate balloons, making them lighter than air. He reasoned that the same principle applied to a human being would eliminate the need for the balloon. Seidlitz powders (a powder of Rochelle salts and baking soda and another powder of tartaric acid, each being dissolved in water separately, then mixed to form an effervescing drink) were then in common use for various indispositions. Here was a gas generating substance that might do the trick. The simple-minded Oates boy was encouraged to drink large quantities of the bubbling mixture with the net result he became extremely ill. Efforts to get the Oates boy airborne concluded somewhat like the previous affair—Al got the

licking but this time only from his mother.

Though Sam Edison thought his son deprived himself of boyhood fun, Al found happiness in his own way. Where other boys enjoyed games and the Port Huron waterfront, his intellectual pursuits were the source of his happiness. He was secluded in a corner of the basement with his chemicals, steam engines and a homemade telegraph key, but who could charge that the boys playing outside were happier?

There were times he would permit the other boys to participate in his newly acquired knowledge. Using an old battery, he would insert one of its wires in a glass of water in which a quarter had been placed. It was understood that anyone who would grasp the handle of the battery with one hand and take the quarter out of the glass of water with the other could have it. To fail would cost the participant a quarter. The strong current generated by the battery was not conducive to success. Al never lost a bet.

THE WEEKLY HERALD. First published by T. A. Edison early in 1862, it was said to be the first newspaper in the world published on a train. Edison National Historic Site.

Electricity fascinated him. His eager interest in telegraphy at the age of eleven had him practicing the Morse code by the hour on his homely telegraph set. No one could answer his question "What is electricity?" Not even an old Scottish line repairman could give him the answer though he tried to explain its action on the telegraph line with the simile "If you had a dog like a Dachshund, long enough to reach from Edinburgh to London—if you pulled his tail in Edinburgh he would bark in London—that is the telegraph." This was partly satisfactory to young Edison but puzzled him as to what went through the dog or over the wire.

Not satisfied with just a sending set, Al also built a receiving set. His satisfaction was incomplete for he had to have someone at the other end of the line. With the assistance of a chum, James Clancy, he built a half-mile line between their houses through a woods. Using stove pipe wire suspended along insulators made from small glass bottles nailed to trees, the telegraph line functioned satisfactorily. Clancy, who often helped him sell newspapers, would send and receive messages by the hour over the improvised telegraph line.

Al's father, who loved to read one of the unsold newspapers each night, had to be quite stern to get Al away from his telegraphic equipment and on to bed.

Al contrived the idea of not bringing home any newspapers, telling his father business had picked up and he had sold out. He suggested that they could get the news each night over the private telegraph wire from Clancy since they always purchased a newspaper. The suggestion was quite acceptable. In this fashion young Edison often stayed up till midnight and later, practicing his Morse code.

The beginning of the Civil War was the beginning of big business for Al. Noticing that newspapers carrying battle reports sold faster than others, he went to the composing room of the Detroit *Free Press* each day to examine the galley proofs. In this way he learned in advance if that day's edition contained battle accounts so that he could take extra papers with him to supply the demand.

In April, 1862, he learned of the Battle of Shiloh before the paper was off the presses. Hurrying to a telegraph operator, he made a deal with him. For wiring a short news bulletin to the telegraphers at each station on the road to Port Huron, and having them chalked up on the depot bulletin boards, the Detroit operator would receive newspaper and magazine subscriptions from Al.

With this assurance of advance publicity, he approached the newspaper's managing editor, Wilbur F. Storey, asking him for 1,000 papers on credit. He usually took 200 papers. Storey listened to the cheeky youngster, then granted him his request. The promotion fared better than Al planned or hoped for. As he told the story:

"When I got to the first station . . . the platform was crowded with men and women. After one look at the crowd I raised the price to ten cents. I sold 35 papers. At Mount Clemens, where I usually sold six papers, the crowd was there too . . . I raised the price from ten cents to fifteen cents . . . . It had been my practice at Port Huron to jump from the train one quarter of a mile from the station where the train generally slackened speed . . . . The little Dutch boy with the horse usually met me there. When the wagon approached the outskirts of town I was met by a large crowd. I then yelled: Twenty-five cents, gentlemen — I haven't enough to go around."

The success of his sale convinced him that "the telegraph was just about the best thing going, for it was the notices on the bulletin that had done the trick. I determined at once to become a telegrapher."

The field of journalism had its lure. Early in 1862 he purchased a small second-hand printing press and some type. He had made the purchase from J. A. Roys, a prominent Detroit bookseller who had obtained the press from the manager of the Cass House—Detroit's finest hotel—for an unpaid debt. At the Cass House it had been used for printing menus. A friend at the Detroit *Free Press* had given Al the type.

Sidetracking his chemicals and his telegrapher's key the moment he set up his press in the baggage car, he used all of his spare moments learning how to operate it. Soon he

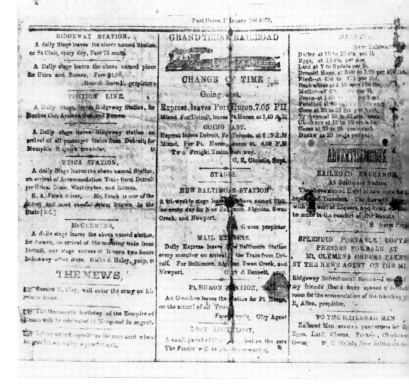

**LOCAL NEWS AND GOSSIP** soon made **The Weekly Herald** a profitable venture. Though the 15-year-old publisher had his problems with grammar and spelling, he knew what his readers' interests were. Edison National Historic Site.

**JAMES URQUHART MACKENZIE** was born in Inverness, Scotland, in 1837. In repayment for saving his son's life, the red bearded Mount Clemens telegrapher taught young Edison the rudiments of his trade—enough so to become a second class operator. 1889. Edison National Historic Site.

began publishing a small newspaper covering local news and general gossip. Probably the first newspaper in the world to be published on a moving train, the *Weekly Herald,* selling at three cents a single copy and eight cents a month, had a regular subscription of nearly 500 and a few hundred in single copies at the peak of its publication. The publisher-editor-printer-newsboy would net about $45 a month from this venture.

One day the train was traveling over a particularly rough section of track when a sudden lurch of the baggage car threw a jar of phosphorus sticks to the floor. The phosphorus, once out of the water and exposed to air, began to ignite, setting fire to the wooden floor of the car. With the aid of the conductor, Alexander Stevenson, the fire was put out but that was the end of the baggage car shelter for Al's equipment and press. Stevenson had no intention of being blown up. He wanted the traveling laboratory removed. Al could do nothing but comply.

The story has been told that Stevenson had thrown young Edison and his equipment off the train on their stop at Smith's Creek station and boxed his ears with such force that deafness soon followed. In later years Edison said that the account of his ears being boxed was untrue. He went on to relate that he had arrived at the station one morning just as the freight was pulling out. Running after it with his arms full of newspapers, he tried to lift himself up on the rear step. "A trainman reached over and grabbed me by the ears and lifted me . . . . I felt something snap inside my head, and the deafness started from that time and has progressed ever since . . . . If it was that man who lifted me by my ears who injured me, he did it to save my life." His intimate friend Henry Ford once wrongly stated that the deafness dated from an operation for mastoiditis, and that he turned this physical problem to his advantage; that his deficiency eliminated many disturbing sounds.

With the impairment of his hearing at the age of twelve there was a tendency to withdraw from society. He became even more serious, even more interested in experimenting and in reading. His interest in the Detroit Public Library increased, the library becoming a refuge. He recalled: "I started with the first book on the bottom shelf and went through the lot, one by one. I didn't read a few books. I read the library. Then I got a collection called *The Penny Library Encyclopedia* and went through that.*" Burton's *Anatomy of Melancholy* and Newton's *Principles* followed, the latter so confusing he developed a permanent distaste for mathematics. His growing deafness provided a certain isolation that gave him the opportunity to think out the many questions that arose from his extensive reading. He was at an impressionable age and there was so much he wanted to know.

Al continued the publishing of his *Weekly Herald* at home. Influenced by an acquaintance who worked in the print shop of the Port Huron *Commercial,* he renamed his publication *Paul Pry.* Its chief subject matter was society news with some emphasis on gossip.

One reader took offense at an item directed toward him and responded by threatening Al with bodily harm. When they did meet, one biographer, Josephson, declares Al was thrown into the St. Clair River, and another, Simonds, would have it that Al dived into the river—the young newspaperman swam for his salvation. In any event *Paul Pry* promptly ceased publication.

One morning late in the summer of 1862, the fifteen-year-old Al was standing on the station platform at Mt. Clemens awaiting the switching of a boxcar. Noticing that three-year-old Jimmy, son of stationmaster J. U. Mackenzie, was playing between the rails in the path of the oncoming boxcar, he cast aside his armful of newspapers, flew to the side of the child and scooped him up in time to avoid certain death.

Tom Sutherland, the train baggageman, who was an eyewitness, told Mackenzie that "had Al been a second later he would have lost a foot or been killed, as the wheel of the car struck the heel of his boot." Though of limited means, the grateful father offered Al any reward within his power.

Al had no immediate answer but Mackenzie remembered seeing him constantly at the side of his telegraph table. On offering to teach him telegraphy—an offer that was accepted immediately—he arranged to board Al during the several months of evening study for the bare cost of the food. Al turned over half of his newspaper business to another boy in order to have more time at the Mt. Clemens stop-off.

After ten days of instruction Al did not show up for several days. When he did return he displayed a complete set of telegraph instruments that operated perfectly. He had made them at

GRAND TRUNK RAILWAY STATION IN MOUNT CLEMENS, MICHIGAN, where young Edison was taught to be a telegrapher. Edison National Historic Site.

the Fisher & Long Gunshop in Detroit. Later he used these same instruments at Bill Hugh's drugstore in Mt. Clemens when he and Rowland Benner constructed a telegraph line between the station and the courthouse square. The wire consisted of annealed iron stovepipe wire nailed to a stake-and-rider-rail fence. Working fairly well in dry weather, it was a flop when conditions were damp or wet. In one month they were out of business; their gross income totaled 37½ cents.

Rowland Benner, Mrs. Mackenzie's brother, was a fellow telegraph student.

For three months Al made his evening stops at Mt. Clemens, learning the techniques of a first class telegrapher. Though he had not acquired an expert's speed of 45 words a minute he was able to abbreviate the railroad telegraphers' signals and send and receive well enough to serve as a "plug" or substitute operator. That background, with the urgent need for operators during the third year of the Civil War, would enable him to find work wherever he might go.

THE EDISON BIRTHPLACE TODAY is a memorial and a museum open to the public. This National Historic Landmark is in Milan, Ohio, two miles south of the Ohio Turnpike using interchange 7. 1947. Courtesy Mrs. John Eyre Sloane.

Following the announcement of his success with the incandescent light he was overrun by people from all over the world eager to contract for its use in their countries — Louis Rau of France, Etienne Fodor of Hungary, Emil Rathenau of Germany, Professor Colombo and Signor Buzzi of Italy, Messieurs Turrettini, Biedermann, and Thury of Switzerland, to name a few. J. W. White photo, Port Huron, Mich. 1892. Edison National Historic Site.

Chapter Three

# Wanderlust

"Who in hell keeps tooting that infernal locomotive whistle?" The question was on everyone's mind in Port Huron that bitter cold morning. A huge ice jam in the St. Clair River had severed all communication, including the ferry service and the telegraph cable between Port Huron and its sister city, Sarnia, Ontario.

Word quickly spread that it was young Tom Edison who was making all the noise. He had encouraged an engineer to bring a locomotive down to the dock and keep up a head of steam while he used the whistle in long and short toots to attract the attention of the Canadians on the opposite shore three-fourths of a mile away. A telegrapher over there, soon grasping the idea that the tooting was in Morse code, had a locomotive driven to the ferry dock where he responded in kind. By creating an emergency communication system, Tom became the talk of two towns.

He had been working in Tom Walker's jewelry and book store for $20 a month principally operating the telegraph key there in the place of the telegrapher who had volunteered for military service. He had started working there in the winter of 1863—the train whistle message service incident took place in early Spring—to obtain experience in telegraphy. There were few messages during the day but each night high-speed press copy would come over the wire for the local newspaper. Tom placed a cot in the rear of the store so he could obtain the experience of receiving these news items when they came through each night.

In May, 1863, he accepted the position of night operator at Stratford Junction, the Grand Trunk Railroad paying him $25 a month. He was now living in Ontario 40 miles from home. Though the 7 p.m. to 7 a.m. shift seemed long, the work was light. He had only to receive messages, then signal trains or stations on a required schedule. Regulations required night operators to report the word *six* every half hour. Inactivity during his nightly vigil made him drowsy. Walking and exploring Stratford was one way to keep awake but he could not walk far with that mandatory message to be sent each half hour. Reading killed some of the time; building mechanical devices helped use up the balance. The last device he made there is of particular interest.

By constructing a notched wheel that he attached to a clock nearby and wired to a main circuit, he had a device that would interrupt the circuit at regular half-hour intervals and spell out *six*. A detective operator exposed young Edison when it was discovered he would not respond to signals between "sixing" signals. A severe reprimand was the result.

Trouble followed Tom. One night not long

**MARSHALL LEFFERTS**, a former Army telegrapher, became the Eastern superintendent of the Western Union Telegraph Company. Lefferts wisely contracted with Edison for his ideas and production of stock tickers. Library of Congress.

**SAMUEL F. B. MORSE**, inventor of the telegraph, at the age of 59. In 1844 he sent his first telegram. By doing so he introduced a practical use for electricity which young Edison found so fascinating not long afterward. 1850. Western Union Telegraph Company.

after his reprimand a rush order came through to hold up a freight train. Rushing out to find the signalman, he was horrified to see the train go by. He hurried into the station and sent a message that the order came too late—the train had passed the station. Edison was informed that the dispatcher had ordered another train through from the opposite direction; the two trains were heading toward each other on a single track.

Realizing that a wreck seemed certain, he "ran toward a lower station near the junction," he recalled, "in a forlorn hope of catching the train. The night was dark, and I fell into a culvert and was knocked senseless." The alert engineers saw each others' headlights when approaching on a straightaway and the accident was averted.

The following day Edison was in the general manager's Toronto office by request. After some pointed questions following a statement that his alleged negligence could mean a prison sentence, the irate manager turned his attention to a business delegation that just had arrived. The boy was badly scared for it seemed that the manager meant business. While the manager talked to his guests Tom slipped out of the office and headed for the railroad. Taking a fast freight to Sarnia and then the ferry to Port Huron, he put both feet on Michigan earth and took one long breath.

The Lake Shore & Michigan Southern Railroad needed an operator at Adrian, Michigan. When Tom took the job, he was assigned to Lenawee Junction some 11 miles from Adrian. He accepted the night "trick" since it gave him more time to experiment. The station agent gave him a small room in the back of the station to use as a shop.

One day he took the day operator's shift so he could take the day off. At nine o'clock that morning the general superintendent handed him a dispatch with orders to break in on the busy line. For ten minutes he attempted to break in but was resisted by the other operator. Ultimately he was successful. Unfortunately the operator he broke in on was the superintendent of telegraph who had been handling the key in the downtown Western Union office. As Edison related the rest of the story, "In about 20 minutes he arrived, livid with rage, and I was discharged on the spot. I informed him that the general superintendent had told me to break in and send the dispatch, but the general superintendent then and there repudiated the whole

**EDISON'S FIRST INVENTION WAS A VOTE RECORDER** no one wanted. This model was demonstrated before a Congressional committee whose chairman advised young Edison congressmen had no wish to hurry up their voting by the accurate and speedy electronic device since it would interfere with their filibustering. This was invented by Edison in Boston in 1868, when he was 21 years old. Edison National Historic Site.

**EDISON'S STOCK TICKER** was referred to as the Edison Universal Printer. This 1871 model, his first commercial invention, was manufactured at his Newark factory. The keyboard consisted of letters—no numerals—operating like a typewriter though receiving as well as sending messages. Edison National Historic Site.

**JAY GOULD** pooled his talents with those of Jim Fisk in an effort to corner the American gold market, then inflate the metal's value to a point where they could sell and reap a fortune. In this they failed, President Grant outmaneuvering them. Gould used Edison's automatic telegraph transmitter in his campaign to take over the nation's telegraph system. Library of Congress.

thing. Their families were socially close, so I was sacrificed. My faith in human nature got a slight jar."

He moved on to Toledo, Ohio, where he secured a day job at Fort Wayne, Indiana, with the Pittsburgh, Fort Wayne & Chicago Railroad. Two months after that found him in Indianapolis at the Union Station working for the Western Union Telegraph Company for $75 a month. It was the fall of 1864. Superintendent Wallick had loaned him some instruments that aided him in developing a telegraphic repeater which one expert considered as "probably the most simple and ingenious arrangement of connections for a repeater."

Ordinary messages were no problem for Tom but news reports for the press were long and, as a result, came fast. Though he practiced diligently, for it was his ambition to take press reports without a break, he "broke" frequently. His solution to the problem was to line up two embossing Morse registers so that one received messages at 50 words a minute and the other would repeat the dots and dashes at 25 words a minute on another strip of paper so he could write the copy neatly and cleanly at his leisure.

The system worked fine—while no one was around—until the speed was increased and the.

equipment was unable to keep up, thereby delaying delivery of the news reports. The newspapers complained of the delay. An investigation revealed the ingenious device and the manager issued an order forbidding its use.

Years later Edison applied the principle to recorders using paper disks on which the indentations would form a volute spiral as they revolved in the same manner disc records do today. He said: "It was this instrument which gave me the idea of the phonograph while working on the telephone."

In February, 1865, he resigned and moved to Cincinnati where he worked in the commercial department of Western Union for $60 a month. Here he was befriended by Milton F. Adams, then 21 years old and a dude by his own statement. Tom was 18, quite unstylish of dress and uncouth of manner. The other operators were somewhat unfriendly but Adams, noticing he was lonesome, offered companionship. They soon became good friends.

Tom spent his spare time manipulating batteries and circuits trying to devise a means of relieving the monotony of telegraphy. This was aided by the pranks he played on his associates by employing the battery circuits.

In a cellar overrun with rats, he arranged two metal plates so that a rat, in placing its forefeet on one and its hindfeet on the other, receiving the full impact of an electrical charge, was electrocuted. This he called his "rat paralyzer."

Tom's thirst for knowledge brought a realization that he could acquire more information only by reading more books. The answer appeared simple: "After I became a telegraph operator I practiced for a long time to become a rapid reader of print, and got so expert I could sense the meaning of a whole line at once. This faculty, I believe, should be taught in schools, as it appears to be easily acquired. Then one can read two or three books in a day, whereas if each word at a time only is sensed reading is laborious."

Still a "plug," Tom kept practicing so he could be rated a first-class operator. He often acted as a night substitute for any operator wishing a few free hours which enabled him to practice taking "press."

One such night when most of the operators were celebrating with a visiting union delegation, Tom was alone trying to keep up with the Cleveland wire. His hand written copy looked good on the unruled paper but the individual

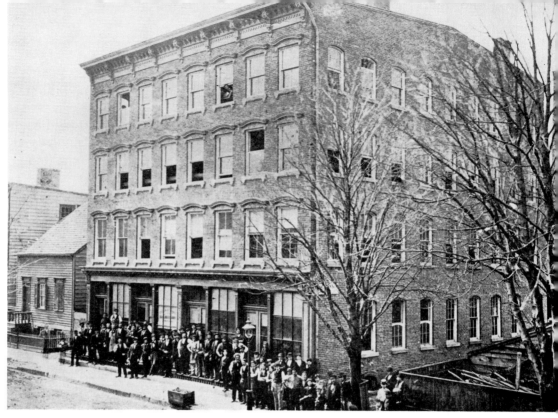

letters of the words would not bear close scrutiny. Words that he missed were filled with illegible scribble he hoped the printers would be able to fill for continuity. When he was through he was too nervous to go home.

When Mr. Stevens, the day manager, arrived, the morning newspapers were out. The press reports in them were perfect. Later in the day Stevens examined the copy on the office hook with apparent satisfaction, then walked over to Tom and said: "Young man, I want you to work the Louisville wire nights; your salary will be $125." His salary had been $80 a month.

The advancement to a first-class operator seemed to encourage Tom to wander. With the war now over he was tempted to see the South. His first move was to Nashville and then on to Memphis, Tennessee. It was at Memphis he perfected his telegraph repeater.

There was no direct wire between New Orleans and New York. Any message was delayed by detours to intervening cities; this required retelegraphing. By perfecting the repeater he had developed at Indianapolis he was able, at Memphis, to connect New York and New Orleans directly. The Memphis *Avalanche* came out with a story on it which was read by the chief operator, a protege of the superintendent. The chief operator had been working on the same problem without success. When Edison returned that afternoon for duty he was discharged without explanation. And the super-intendent refused to issue a rail pass to Memphis.

Despite a fair salary Tom had very little money. He had been spending freely on books and electrical equipment with which to experiment. Near starvation at Decatur, Alabama, he had to stay three days before moving north to Nashville. There at the telegraph office he secured a pass to Louisville and enough money to buy a square meal. Arriving in Louisville in the middle of a snowstorm, and clad in a linen duster, he managed to find work at the Western Union office. His old friend Adams had said of him, "as an operator he had no superior and very few equals," so he managed to hold his job there for more than a year.

Obtaining a furnished room on Third Street not far from the telegraph office, he soon converted it into a laboratory. One day about 3 a.m. he was walking down a dark street to his room with a large bundle of used magazines slung over his back when he became conscious of bullets flying by his head. He had not heard a policeman call to him nor had he heard the firing. The law officer was mortified when his examination revealed nothing but old magazines.

Tom had an interest in everything. By constant reading he knew what went on politically and internationally. He would follow the speeches of all political candidates and was never neutral in his political opinions. Though

**THE EMBOSSING TELEGRAPH,** sometimes called the repeating telegraph, was said by Edison to be the father of the phonograph. Edison National Historic Site.

he would not go out of his way to offend anyone, he was not hesitant to give an opposing opinion if he had one. Since he rarely slept more than four or five hours he read newspapers for several hours each day and kept posted on all current matters.

Frequently the telegraph wires were old and uninsulated. In stormy weather he would receive incomplete dispatches. Drawing from memory he would supply missing words and sometimes entire sentences.

He experimented with various forms of handwriting. With messages coming at the rate of 35 to 40 a minute he found it necessary to write fast and legibly. The result was a vertical script without any flourishes and in which each letter was separate. Taking eight to 15 columns of news each day, he soon was able to write 55 words a minute—a speed faster than a telegraph operator could send.

During the Civil War and immediately after,

**THIS MODEL OF THE FIRST TYPEWRITER** was brought to Edison's Newark shop by its inventor, Christopher L. Sholes, for Edison's assistance in making it commercially useful. Its letters would wander out of alignment, a fault soon corrected. It became the forerunner of the Remington typewriter. Edison National Historic Site.

operators were few. The average operator received between $70 and $90 a month, the average work day ranging from 10 to 15 hours. There was no sick pay and most operators worked Sundays. The telegraph offices were dark, dirty and badly equipped. Western Union along with some other companies made tremendous profits.

Edison's propensity for experimenting with the company wires and equipment was most annoying to the Louisville office manager. Tom had been forbidden to touch any company equipment except in the course of his duties. But he was absorbed with ideas in the area of automatic telegraphy. Needing some sulphuric acid, he ignored an order against visiting the battery room. The carboy tipped over and spilled the acid. Leaking through to the manager's room below, it ate up his desk and carpet. The following day Tom was fired.

Back to Cincinnati he went. While there he became quite friendly with Mr. Sommers, the superintendent of telegraph for the Cincinnati & Indianapolis Railroad. Sommers provided Tom with scrap materials that were quite useful in his experimentation and the two began working together on a self-adjusting relay. Both enjoyed practical jokes.

Tom acquired a second-hand Ruhmkorff induction coil which was strong enough to contract arm and hand muscles so a man couldn't let go of it. One day the two of them visited the roundhouse. After connecting one electrode to the wash tank and grounding the other in the earth, they crawled onto the flat roof of the washroom where they had bored a hole in the roof. From this vantagepoint they observed a man walk in and stand on the wet floor as he dipped his hands in the wash water. Up flew his hands. Trying again with the same result, he stood by the wall with a puzzled expression on his face. Soon another victim approached and received the same shock. The two left. Soon a crowd gathered in the room, the trick having caused considerable excitement for no one was able to explain what was happening. Sommers and Edison enjoyed the scenes enormously.

Always industrious in his spare time, Tom had taught himself to read, write and speak French from a French-English dictionary. Early in 1867 he began to learn Spanish in the same fashion in preparation for going to Brazil. Two young Southerners had encouraged him to join them in a trip to Brazil where the government was offering large salaries to experienced telegraphers. A network of telegraph lines was being constructed in the Brazilian jungles.

Tom hurried home to visit his mother at Port Huron before leaving the country. Attempts to discourage him were useless. He returned to Louisville where he met his friends, then traveled on to New Orleans. But the steamship chartered to transport them, along with a large number of former Confederate officers, was delayed because of a local political upheaval.

A chance meeting with a former resident of South America provided him with an anything but inviting picture. His interest in the trip cooled so he returned to Louisville where he procured his former job. Late in the fall of 1867 he returned to Port Huron, broke and jobless as before.

Soon becoming restless, Edison wrote to his friend Milton Adams in Boston to see if any jobs were available. Adams asked the Western Union office manager, George F. Milliken, if there was an opening for a good operator. Milliken cautiously asked if the man in question made good copy. Adams showed him Edison's letter in its script handwriting. When asked if the writer could take it off the line as well, Adams assured him that "there was nobody who could stick him." Milliken told Adams he could send for Edison.

Tom had no money for fare. He had helped out the Grand Trunk Railroad telegraph people by devising a way of using one submarine cable so it would serve the place of two, since one of their two cables had been lost. He thought he was entitled to a railroad pass and they agreed.

In March of 1868 he arrived in Boston. His trip had been eventful for he had been delayed by being on a snowbound train in Canada for most of a week.

Bronze bust of Thomas Alva Edison. 1885. By Walter Stevens. Edison National Historic Site.

**WESTERN UNION TELEGRAPH COMPANY "RECEIPTS AND EXPENSES"** of the Indianapolis Office showing T. A. Edison on its payroll during November and December, 1864, and January, 1865. Edison National Historic Site.

January 1865.

| Dr. | | Cr. | |
|---|---|---|---|
| amt. Brot. Forward | 1412 24 | Paid other Lines | 6 37 |
| Receipts for Jany. | 2275 29 | 1 Chas. C. Whitney | 110 00 |
| from Assd. Press | 339 00 | 2 R. C. Duncan | 110 00 |
| From Union Railway Co. | | 3 F. L. Smith | 90 00 |
| account Salary | 90 00 | 4 E. L. Parmelee | 85 00 |
| | | 5 A. Brewer | 85 00 |
| | | 6 J. A. Edison | 75 00 |
| | | 7 J. A. Ramsay | 75 00 |
| | | 8 | |

Edison would help a worthy man help himself but did not believe in charity. J. W. White photo, Port Huron, Mich. 1892. Edison National Historic Site.

Chapter Four

# A Beginning In Boston

The boys were ready for the rube from the Midwest. Knowing that the main wire from New York would be assigned to him, they had arranged to have one of the fastest telegraphers in New York send him press copy for the Boston *Herald*.

When Tom arrived he was dressed in an unstylish, wide-brimmed hat, baggy, shabby clothes, long hair, and a plug of tobacco bulging in one cheek.

The Western Union's office manager, George F. Milliken, had interviewed him earlier that day and, after a five-minute interview, had given him a job starting at 5:30 p.m.

Once he was seated at his instruments the New York telegrapher began sending slowly, then increasing his speed, "to which," Edison said, "I easily adapted my pace." By the amused and excited appearance of those around him, Tom knew he was in a put-up job. The New Yorker then began slurring words, running them together, even sticking signals, in an effort to upset Tom. This was old stuff to Tom. When he thought the fun had gone far enough, for he had about completed the special press report, he opened the key and clicked out," Say, young man, change off and send with your other foot." The man at the other end of the line couldn't finish his work.

Tom's interest in electricity continued. And his interest in improving telegraphy equipment never flagged. The many Boston bookstores were frequented by him in an effort to obtain any available books on the subject. In one he purchased a two-volume set of Michael Faraday's *Experimental Researches in Electricity*. He repeated all of the experiments in the volumes, coming to the conclusion that Faraday was the master experimenter. The explanations were simple for Faraday used no mathematics, much to Tom's satisfaction.

Telegraphy to Tom was a means to an end —a remunerative occupation. His first interest had been curiosity. Continuous occupation with telegraphy incurred a sort of boredom for his inordinately active mind. His job severances invariably emanated from his refusal to follow a set office routine or discipline. He would allow outgoing messages to pile up for hours if he was preoccupied with reading or drawing. If an idea came to him while receiving, he would signal the other operator to wait, meanwhile using his notebook, then would signal the operator to continue.

Though constantly striving to contrive some device that would make telegraphy less irksome, he had his moments for fun. He loved to devise a gadget that could be used to play a practical joke on someone.

The operators had a bad habit of carrying

away the tin dipper hung over a tank of ice water. Tom wired the nail the dipper hung on to a 190 cell Fuller battery. Nearby was a sign: "Please return the dipper." Thereafter it was heeded by everyone. No one was able to remove the dipper while the battery was attached, and there were a dozen sore arms in the office to attest to its shocking qualities.

In a practical approach to an office nuisance he was able to indulge in some humor. The telegraph office previously had been a restaurant. This was evident at lunch time when the cockroaches left their domicile under the baseboards. Tom pasted two strips of tin-foil on the wall, connecting one piece to a negative pole of a large battery used for the telegraph wires and the other to the positive pole. When the cockroaches moved up the wall, the moment they walked over the strips, they literally exploded into a gas. He remarked: "This automatic electrocuting device got half a column in an evening paper, and attracted so much attention that the manager made me stop it."

The principal of a fashionable young ladies school called at the Western Union office one day to request that a demonstration and an explanation of telegraphy be given at her school. Tom accepted the assignment but, in doing so,

**WILLIAM LESLIE EDISON AND THOMAS A. EDISON JR.** Left to right. Ca. 1883. Sarony photo, New York. Edison National Historic Site.

**MRS. MARY STILWELL EDISON** was the inventor's first wife. They were married December 25, 1871, in Newark. Ca. 1883. Sarony photo, New York. Edison National Historic Site.

**TO MRS. MARY STILLWELL EDISON** a daughter, Marion, was born in 1873; a son, Thomas Jr., in 1876; and another son, William Leslie, in 1878. Marion was nicknamed Dot, and Thomas Jr., Dash, to commemorate his time-consuming interest in telegraphy. Ca. 1882. Batchelor collection, Edison National Historic Site.

invited Adams along. The two rigged up wires across the schoolroom, one end being on the stage that young Edison occupied. When the door opened and about 20 elegantly dressed young ladies filed in, the flabbergasted Tom managed to gasp out that he would work the equipment and Mr. Adams would give the explanation. Though both told the story differently afterward, it appears that Adams became so embarrassed he fell over a stool. The giggling of the girls made him speechless. In desperation, Edison, who was equally bashful, proceeded with the explanation. He was never able to understand why it was the best talk of his entire life.

Aside from being paid for the demonstration Tom was the recipient of a fringe benefit. There were times, when walking down the street with other operators, he would meet some of these young ladies. The nods and smiles they gave him were a source of mystery to his companions and a great boost to his ego.

The boredom and monotony of the long hours in the telegraph office were broken by his hours of experimentation and reading. While experimenting with a large induction coil he accidentally took hold of both electrodes. The muscular contraction was so great he was unable to let go. To free himself he backed away from the coil so the battery wires would pull the batteries off the shelf and break the circuit. Fortunately he shut his eyes as he gave the last pull for the nitric acid in the batteries splashed onto his face. Rushing to the sink, he climbed in and poured water over his head to dilute the acid and stop the intense pain of the burn. As he related, "When I finally looked at myself in the glass I was a ghastly black and yellow—my skin was thoroughly oxidized. It

**THE AUTOMATIC TELEGRAPH APPARATUS,** completed in 1872, was Edison's answer to high-speed telegraphy. Lord Kelvin recommended it for an award at the 1876 Centennial Exposition in Philadelphia "as a very important step in land telegraphy." Edison National Historic Site.

was two weeks before I could go out in the street again. My face looked dreadful. My eyes, fortunately, had been closed when the accident took place or I would have been blinded."

Boston had become somewhat of a center for those who were interested in dabbling or investigating along scientific lines. Tom had discovered that Court Street was the location for clockmakers, opticians and other skilled tradesmen. He soon came across the electrical workshop of Charles Williams Jr., where some of the first fire-alarms in America were being manufactured and where Alexander Graham Bell would develop the telephone.

It didn't take Tom long to arrange for a corner in the Williams shop. There he could experiment daily and be near others who bub-

**EDISON PEERING INTO HIS BLACK BOX** where two adjustable graphite points, separated and placed in circuit with a vibrating telegraphic coil, can be seen to emit an unusual spark. This spark, unlike any other he was familiar with, he first observed on November 22, 1875. Not able to determine the cause of this "etheric force" as he called it, he soon used induction to send messages without wires from his laboratory to his residence. From this he obtained the first patents on aerials and antennas and a method of sending messages from a moving train. Edison National Historic Site.

**MARION ESTELLE EDISON.** Ca. 1880-1881. C. Parker photo. Newark, N. J. Edison National Historic Site.

**MARION ESTELLE EDISON** was born in 1873. Ca. 1878. C. Parker photo, Newark, N. J. Edison National Historic Site.

bled with ideas. The town was filled with embryonic and hopeful inventors.

About this time Tom read in a scientific journal that Alfred Nobel, a Swedish scientist, had developed a technique of preparing nitroglycerin. Fired by the thought of making some, he read the details of the method carefully so he could compound it. Williams too was excited by the idea so the two concocted some. While testing a very small quantity, the explosion it produced caused them considerable alarm. As Edison said, "The fact dawned upon us that we had a very white elephant in our possession."

Early the next morning Tom put the explosive in a soft drink bottle, wrapped it in paper and then tying a string to it, gently lowered it into a sewer at the corner of State and Washington Streets. Another explosion in the accumulated sewer gas could have started America's first urban renewal project.

In June, 1868, *The Journal of the Telegraph* carried an article on Edison in reference to an "interesting, simple and ingenious" invention, a "mode of transmission both ways on a single wire." His friend Adams had signed the article though Tom had prompted and directed it.

Copies were sent to former colleagues who had scorned his experiments. Actually his findings were of no great importance; they were merely refinements on existing equipment. More important was the response from some who offered to back his experiments with small amounts of capital. This encouraged him to consider giving up telegraphy and utilizing his entire time in research.

He had been working in the Williams workshop on an idea that would, so he hoped, be the means of financial independence and a permanent break from the telegraph office. This first invention, known as a vote recorder, resulted in a patent application on October 11, 1868. The patent was granted June 1, 1869.

Backed with a small amount of capital three Boston "investors" had provided, Tom had made a model vote recorder to use as a demonstrator before a committee of the United States Congress. He had observed that "an enormous amount of time was wasted during each session of the House in foolishly calling the members' names and recording, and then adding their votes, when the whole operation could be done in almost a moment by merely pressing a particular button at each desk."

The chairman of the committee on observing

the ease and accuracy of the device commented, "Young man, if there is any invention on earth that we don't want down here it is this . . . fili-bustering and delay on the counting of votes are often the means we have for defeating bad legis-lation."

When Edison returned home he remarked philosophically, "But it was a lesson to me. There and then I made the vow I would never invent anything which was not wanted, or which was not necessary to the community at large."

Just the year before—in 1867—E. A. Calla-han had invented a stock ticker and had placed it in service in New York. Tom started work on an alphabetic type wheel instrument that could be used for telegraphy between business concerns. His improvement on the Callahan equipment did away with the need for an oper-ator at the subscriber's end of the wire and also reduced much of the wire used.

On January 25, 1869, he applied for a patent on this improved stock ticker; his second patent application.

A small company had been formed to pro-mote the ticker and in a short time there were 30 subscribers. A disagreement ended in the sale of the patent rights to a large telegraph

**MARION ESTELLE EDISON.** Ca. 1883. Sarony photo, New York. Edison National Historic Site.

**WILLIAM LESLIE EDISON** was born in 1878. Ca. 1881. C. Parker photo, Newark, N. J. Edison National Historic Site.

**THOMAS A. EDISON JR.** was born in 1876. Ca. 1878. C. Parker photo, Newark, N. J. Edison National Historic Site.

company. Edison derived very little in the settlement.

The offerings of financial backing to his experiments were encouragement enough to cause him to express his exuberance in a bit of practical joking in the telegraph office. Treating the receipt of stock market quotations as trivial by copying them in such fine handwriting 2,000 words covered a single page of paper, he received a protest from the night manager. If the words were too small he would make them larger. Using lettering so large it took a full page to hold one or two words, and a bundle several feet thick for an entire message, he was near to being assaulted by the newspaper's press foreman. A demotion from the press table to sending only, followed. Edison promptly resigned.

In January, 1869, he gave public notice he would devote full time to inventing. A statement in a telegraphic trade journal made the announcement. An advertisement drew attention to a double transmitter he made available at $400 each, and that he was located at 109 Court Street, the shop of Charles Williams, Jr. Now associated with George Anders as a free-lance inventor, he had struck out on his own, at age 21.

Continuing his work on the duplex telegraph, he borrowed $800 from E. B. Welch, giving him a personal note and a signed agree-

**THE FIRST MIMEOGRAPH** was Edison's electric pen. A. B. Dick of Chicago regarded Edison as the grandfather of all stencil duplication. The A. B. Dick Company bought the invention in 1887 though the Western Electric Company made quite a business of selling the pens earlier. Edison National Historic Site.

ment for a large share of any profits; all on the basis of a trial on the Atlantic & Pacific Telegraph Company lines between Rochester and New York City.

In this attempt to demonstrate the sending of two messages in opposite directions at the same time on a single wire—this was duplex telegraphy—the telegrapher at the New York end of the line apparently failed to do his part though the trial was repeated several mornings in succession (April, 1869).

Now heavily in debt in Boston, and having received encouragement from an electrical engineer in New York to try the big city, he borrowed a few dollars from a friend and took off by boat.

**THE ELECTRIC PEN** was the first commercially manufactured device to employ an electric motor. It was first patented in 1876. The needle point of the pen was driven by a tiny motor at the rate of 8,000 punctures a minute, the power source being two wet-cell batteries. By "writing" on a sheet of wax paper, then passing a felt roller saturated with printer's ink over it, the ink is forced through the perforations onto a sheet of paper below it. Edison National Historic Site.

Chapter Five

# Inventing Was His Business

New York was his oyster. Tom had left all of his possessions behind because he could not afford to bring them along. In addition, he was penniless and hungry. In searching for a solution to his hunger, a wholesale tea warehouse attracted his attention for a "tea taster" could be seen at his work. Tom asked him if he might sample the tea, a request that was complied with. It was Tom's first breakfast in New York.

Near the end of that day he located a telegraph operator he had known but found him unemployed. He did loan Edison a dollar, a small portion of which was promptly used for apple dumplings and coffee at Smith & McNeill's restaurant.

The Western Union's telegraph office was his next stop. There were no vacancies so he decided to call at the office of the Gold Indicator Company. It was a long walk to Broad Street but once at the office he managed to talk to Franklin L. Pope, an electrical engineer and telegraph expert. Pope knew of Edison's efforts in developing a stock ticker in Boston. Realizing Tom's dilemma Pope offered him a cot in the company's battery room temporarily.

Right after the Civil War gold was the standard of exchange, being regarded as much more valuable than paper money. A gold dollar often purchased values greater than a paper dollar, values ranging from a dollar and a quarter to a dollar and a half. Speculation in gold was flourishing at this time and to such an extent that a "Gold Room" had been established on Wall Street. At first this room displayed a blackboard on which the gold prices were shown. This method drew criticism from the brokers as being too slow.

In 1866, Dr. S. S. Laws, vice president and presiding officer of the exchange had initiated a better idea. Beginning in 1865, he had been using a telegraph key to operate an electrical indicator in the Gold Room where price changes could be shown on a central board. Laws' new idea was to use the indicator as a means of transmitting telegraphic impulses by wire to the various brokers who would receive them on an instrument dial. Laws' Gold Indicator Company service was eminently successful, 300 brokers subscribing.

During June, 1869, while Edison was examining the mechanism of Laws' Gold Indicator, the central instrument that sent out quotations, it suddenly stopped functioning. Pandemonium was the result. In a few minutes a boy from the office of each of the 300 brokers had crowded into the office excitedly shouting that their wires had stopped functioning.

Pope lost his head in the excitement and finally his speech. Dr. Laws, almost as excited, could get no response from Pope. He saw his

**EDISON'S MENLO PARK LABORATORY IN THE WINTER OF 1880** is the long building in the center. This first of the group of buildings shown was constructed by early summer of 1876 in the hamlet of Menlo Park, New Jersey, about 25 miles from New York City. Sketch by R. F. Outcault. Edison National Historic Site.

$300,000 a year business about to topple for it was a period in which the price of gold was fluctuating crazily.

Oblivious to the excitement, Edison quietly surveyed the instrument, then went to Laws and Pope telling them he believed he had found the trouble. "Fix it! Fix it! Be quick!" was Laws' response. Tom removed a contact spring that had fallen between two gears, made some minor adjustments and in two hours had things working in fine order.

In a discussion that followed, Laws offered Edison the largest salary he had yet received. His job was to work on and maintain the plant equipment, acting as Pope's assistant.

The following month Pope resigned to go into business as a consultant. Edison took his place at $300 a month. By August he applied for a patent on an improvement of his printing telegraph, and in September another application

**FRONT VIEW OF MENLO PARK LABORATORY ABOUT 1879.** Edison attemped to obtain rural seclusion here, but his inventions of the carbon transmitter, the phonograph, the incandescent lamp and the dynamo drew throngs of curious visitors. Edison National Historic Site.

was made for an additional improvement, but now in partnership with Pope.

During this period, Jay Gould and James Fiske, heading the "Erie Railroad Ring," were trying to corner the gold market. The Government was obtaining its import duties in gold, thereby helping to create a shortage of the precious metal. In turn it was selling $1,000,000 worth each month to help relieve the squeeze.

President Grant had been persuaded to suspend the sale of gold for awhile in the hope it would relieve the pressure. While Grant visited friends in Pennsylvania, well away from all contact with governmental and business affairs, the Gould pool gained control of $10,000,000 in gold. Immediately the price rose to 144; their objective was 200.

On "Black Friday," September 24, 1869, the pool purchased $28,000,000 in gold at 160, driving prices higher. A business panic was imminent though this was of no concern to the Gould interests who saw millions in profit before them. They were forcing a great inflationary boom across the nation, causing the dollar to fall in value correspondingly. There was no federal law or control that could interfere.

In response to urgent requests, President Grant returned to Washington. Toward the end of the day he ordered the U. S. Treasury to sell $4,000,000 of its gold reserve. The reaction on the market was that of relief, the price of gold taking a marked drop to 132.

The Gold Indicator had been so improved by young Edison it rivaled the Gold & Stock Telegraph, the newly acquired possession of Western Union. Laws received an offer from the Western Union to consolidate which he promptly accepted, and then retired. General Marshall Lefferts, the president of the new company, offered to retain Edison in his same capacity but he had other ideas that would give him more independence.

One week later—October 1, 1869—*The Telegrapher* published a half-page advertisement announcing that Pope, Edison & Company would undertake construction of "various types of electrical devices and apparatus" pertaining to telegraphy as well as to build lines or conduct tests. J. A. Ashley, publisher of *The Telegrapher,* was a silent partner, his contribution being advertising space.

Edison boarded at Pope's home in Elizabeth, New Jersey, their shop being a rented one near the Pennsylvania Railroad yards in Jersey City.

Catching a seven o'clock train to Jersey City each morning, working until near one o'clock that night and returning by train was a routine he maintained during the winter of 1870.

Occupying another part of the same shop was a Dr. Bradley who was experimenting with the galvanometer. Curious to know the cause of the horrible stench that constantly emanated from that area, Edison examined the room during Bradley's absence. He discovered that the doctor was attempting to age whiskey by passing a galvanic current through platinum electrodes immersed in the raw fluid. The electrodes were held in place by hard rubber containing sulphur which was producing hydrogen sulphide and the stench of rotten eggs.

The new company was devoting time to the improvement of telegraphy. Edison, working hard on a variation of the printing telegraph, perfected a "gold printer" for reporting gold and silver quotations. His company manufactured and rented the machine for $25 a week, underselling its competitor, the Western Union. Within six months Western Union eliminated this competition by buying it for $15,000, Edison receiving $5,000 for his one-third interest.

By the summer of 1870 he had taken out seven patents affecting telegraphic communication. He was beginning to resent the three-way split of all profits by "doing all the work with compensation narrowed down to the point of extinguishment by the superior business abilities of my partners." He had done most of the work while Ashley had invested no capital and aided in no other way. It was then the partnership dissolved, parting in a friendly manner.

Tom now realized that Western Union would buy out anything competitive. It had a $41,000,000 capitalization and had absorbed many lesser firms in its effort to control the industry. When General Lefferts asked Tom to join his technical staff and improve on Callahan's stock printer, he agreed. No salary was mentioned and no agreement was reached as to who would retain any patents resulting.

In just three weeks he demonstrated a device before the company board of directors that would stop all brokers' tickers in unison, then correct any deviations or errors. Even Callahan, the original inventor of the ticker, admitted that any ticker not having the unison correcting device would be obsolete.

At this point Lefferts offered to settle with Edison. Tom was slow to respond for he was

**SECOND FLOOR OF MENLO PARK LABORATORY IN 1878.** Charles Batchelor faces left front window; Sam Edison stands at side of rear window. Small table in center foreground holds models of Edison's phonographs. April 5, 1878. Photo by S. A. Holmes, New York, Edison National Historic Site.

uncertain as to the amount he should request. To his way of thinking $5,000 would have been acceptable but he would take $3,000. In desperation he asked the General to make him an offer. Lefferts replied, "How would $40,000 strike you?" The near-fainting youth managed to accept the offer.

Three days later he was paid by a check—the first he had ever received. At the bank the teller returned the check to him with some comment he couldn't hear. Thinking he had been cheated, he returned to the General. Lefferts and his secretary, after a good laugh, explained that the check must be endorsed, then the secretary returned with him to the bank to identify him.

The bank teller, seeing the humor in the transaction, paid Edison in 10 and 20-dollar bills that made a stack a foot thick. Stuffing his pockets from his overcoat in, Tom headed for

**GOOD MEN AND TRUE.** Edison sits in the center of his workmen, straw hat on his lap, in front of his laboratory at Menlo Park. 1880. Edison National Historic Site.

**FIRST MACHINE SHOP IN MENLO PARK** was located in the back half of the first floor of the laboratory. Photo taken prior to April 5, 1878. Edison National Historic Site.

**EDISON AND HIS STAFF AT MENLO PARK IN 1880.** Left to right, standing: Albert B. Herrick, Francis Jehl, Samuel "Dad" Edison, George Crosby, George E. Carman, Charles P. Mott, John W. Lawson, George Hill, Ludwig K. Boehm; left to right, seated on chairs: Charles Batchelor, Thomas A. Edison, Charles T. Hughes, William Carman; left to right, seated on steps: William Holzer, James Hipple. Edison National Historic Site.

Newark, staying up all of the night in fear of being robbed. The next morning saw him at the General's office to ask for advice. The General arranged a deposit in the bank.

Tom now was on his own again but this time with money in his pocket. He had an order from Western Union for 1,200 stock tickers—a half million dollar order—he must manufacture in the next few years.

The winter of 1871 was used to survey the industrial area of Newark, New Jersey, for a place to produce his new tickers. The third floor of a building on Ward Street was selected. Applying himself to the task of purchasing equipment, he was nearly out of funds within 30 days.

Several times he had written his parents admonishing them to take it easier and to draw on him for any necessary funds to do so. He had been unable to go home for three years though he was greatly concerned over his mother's failing health and his father's hard labors.

While in the middle of his preparations to equip his new shop a telegram arrived informing him that his mother had passed away in Gratiot village on April 9, 1871, at the age of 61. Though the message arrived two days after her death, he managed to arrive in Port Huron in time for the funeral. The feeling of loss was deep and for years afterward he hardly could speak of her and then to say, "The memory of her will always be a blessing to me."

Back in Newark he soon found out his quarters were too small. More room was available down the street where his original work force of 18 was increased to 50 men, and then 150. He had to put on a night shift, acting as his own foreman on both shifts.

Sleep to him was only an intermission from his work. Seemingly tireless when deeply engrossed in something, he would keep on until his mind ceased to function. When that point arrived he would go to sleep. He might go home to do so, or sleep in his shop, either on a work bench or a cot, if he wished to remain near his project. He never dreamed but went to sleep instantly. He would sleep a half hour or 12 hours, or would go entirely without sleep, depending upon his need. A half-hour nap in each eight hours ofttimes sufficed.

Though Edison seemingly had broken away from the Western Union empire it still had strings tied to him. General Lefferts had seen to it by providing Edison with a partner, a William Unger. Known as the firm of Edison

**SECOND FLOOR OF MENLO PARK LABORATORY IN 1880.**
Left to right: Ludwig K. Boehm, Charles L. Clarke, Charles
Batchelor, William Carman, Samuel D. Mott, George Dean,
Thomas A. Edison (wearing cap), Charles T. Hughes, George
Hill, George E. Carman, Francis Jehl, John W. Lawson,
Charles Flammer, Charles P. Mott and J. U. Mackenzie who
taught Edison telegraphy. The old gas fixtures display in-
candescent lamps. February 22, 1880. Edison National His-
toric Site.

**A GROUP OF MENLO PARK ASSISTANTS IN FRONT OF
THE LABORATORY** in 1880. Left to right, standing: J. Ayers,
James Hipple, unidentified, George Dean, William J. Ham-
mer, John Lawson, Samuel Mott, Thomas A. Edison (with
hands in pockets and wearing a cap), William Holzer, Dr.
Otto Moses, three unidentified men; left to right, seated: C.
Van Cleve, William Mills, William Carman, George Hill and
M. Isaacs. Edison National Historic Site.

**SARAH JORDAN BOARDING HOUSE** where important visitors dined and many of Edison's men roomed. Mrs. Sarah Jordan was related to Edison's first wife, Mary Stillwell. Left to right, standing in yard: Alexander Mungle (in gateway), Anton Westerdahl (back of gate), William Mills, Dick Hickman, T. A. Edison Jr. (standing by tree), Thomas Logan, John Randolph, H. A. Campbell, John Raymon, a maid; left to right, second row: J. W. Lawson (looking from window), W. J. Hammer, Laura Jordan, Mrs. Sarah Jordan, William Holzer, Frank Holzer, Axel K. Westerdahl (Anton's brother). 1880. William J. Hammer collection, Smithsonian Institution.

**EDISON RESIDENCE AT MENLO PARK IN 1881.** Edison National Historic Site.

& Unger, it dissolved a year later probably because of Edison's propensity for bewildering business practices.

He had organized a third small factory in Newark in 1871, in partnership with George Harrington. The Edison & Harrington firm manufactured automatic printing telegraphs but here again trouble developed between the partners. Harrington had interfered with Edison's supervision of the production by placing a man over him as superintendent. Tom walked out.

Some months later they came to an agreement: Edison would not be interfered with in either production or experimentation. His principal interest in Harrington afterward seemed to be that of obtaining money from him when the need was apparent.

Edison had a need for men who were skilled craftsmen. His first were machinists and watchmakers. He had no standard in hiring. Mechanical ability and the capacity to work long periods without sleep were qualities that appealed to him. A fine toolmaker getting $21.50 a week was offered $60 a week to be foreman of both shifts because Edison observed that he worked most of every 24 hours. The man displayed unusual executive ability. In three months production was doubled with but a slight increase in the payroll. For rest he would sleep on the work bench for 20 or 30 minutes, and arise afresh. One day he disappeared. In two weeks he reappeared, unkempt and disheveled. Once seated he said, "Edison, it's no use; this is the third time; I can't stand prosperity. Put my salary back and give me a job." Edison did as he asked and he stayed with him a long time at a lesser job. Whiskey had been his ruin.

It is significant that Edison discovered men at that time who became prominent and wealthy in their own right later on. Sigmund Bergmann, a German Jew who hardly spoke English, was made an inspector soon after he was hired; he paid little attention to the clock. Another German, Johann Schuckert, was an ingenious craftsman. For awhile Bergmann was Edison's partner in some lighting projects. Bergmann and Schuckert finally returned to Germany where they established two of the largest electrical manufacturing corporations in all Europe.

Swiss-born "Honest" John Kruesi was another of Edison's stalwarts. A highly skilled and exceedingly well-trained clockmaker, he could turn any of Edison's sketches into instru-

A PEEK AT MENLO PARK soon after the invention of the incandescent lamp. Left to right: brick building that houses office and library; Charles Dean's house; Mrs. Jordan's boarding house; Edison barn; windmill; Edison residence. 1880. Edison National Historic Site.

ments or equipment.

Then there was John F. Ott. John, at the age of 21, asked for a job. When an unassembled heap of stock printer parts was pointed to and he was asked if he could make them operate, he replied, "You needn't pay me if I don't." Edison hired him on the spot, making him a kind of assistant foreman.

Charles Batchelor, an English draftsman, joined him at this time and evidenced considerable mechanical skill.

Edison displayed a rather unique business attitude. His men were paid for piecework which permitted them to make good money. Since he kept no books he kept his accounts on the hooks: all bills and accounts owed were stuck on one hook; everything owed him was placed an another hook. In lieu of money he gave promissory notes until he could deliver tickers to obtain enough to pay off the notes. Though he managed to maintain his credit he had many protests over this rather unorthodox system.

A bookkeeper was inevitable though more worrisome than his own method of accounting. When the bookkeeper reported they had a surplus of $3,000, Edison celebrated by providing a dinner for some of his men. Two days later the bookkeeper told him there had been an error; that they were in the red $500. A few days after that he disclosed that he was confused, that he had discovered they had made $7,000. This was too much for Edison. He discharged the bookkeeper and vowed never again to regard any excess money as profit until all bills were paid.

Edison had had no time for women in his 24

Sketch of Edison by James Edward Kelly, May 16, 1878, showing the inventor at his tinfoil phonograph. Edison National Historic Site.

speeches that were given and, after he had read a few, he lost all feeling of regret. When he read that a scientist had invented a short-term anesthetic his first thought was of its great value if it could be administered at banquets to people with good hearing.

In later years he attributed to deafness his perfecting the phonograph and his improvement of the telephone. He said he hadn't heard a bird sing since he was 12 years old but could hear anything upon the phonograph. And, fortunately, his eyes always were extremely good.

Discussing his deafness in later years he observed, "It may be said that I was shut off from that particular kind of social intercourse which is small talk. I am glad of it . . . . I have no doubt that my nerves are stronger and better today than they would have been if I had heard all the foolish conversation and other meaningless sounds that normal people hear."

In courtship his deafness was of considerable assistance. It was an excuse to get a little closer than usual, which helped overcome his natural bashfulness. As he said, "After things were actually going a little nicer, I found hearing unnecessary."

There are varying accounts of his courtship to his first wife, Mary Stilwell. One states that he noticed the attractive, well-proportioned 16-year-old girl working in his shop. Another, that two schoolgirls, Alice and Mary Stilwell, took refuge in the shop doorway one afternoon during a pouring rain. Edison was attracted by the vivacity and charm of the youngest one, Mary, and asked her parents' permission to call upon her.

Since both girls taught Sunday school in Newark he had no difficulty getting his friend and partner Joseph T. Murray to accompany him to the church to bring the girls home in a carriage they had hired. Soon afterward he asked Mary's father for her hand in marriage but was told she must wait a year for she was but 16.

Mary, now through with schooling, accepted Tom's offer to assist in his paraffin paper experiments. They were married December 25, 1871, when he was 24.

Though it is told a friend found him in his shop at midnight of his wedding day deep in experiments, it really was a honeymoon of a different nature. It was Tom's plan to take a boat trip to Boston. After his purchase of the tickets for the trip Mary refused to go unless her sister and Joe Murray went along, and

years; his mother, yes, but now she was gone. Perhaps the thought of her made him look at young ladies differently. His natural bashfulness augmented by his deafness caused him to shy away from the opposite sex. In many respects he used his deafness as an asset. It was so in business; over the years he did not rely on verbal reports or agreements, there being too much chance he might not hear them perfectly, so he received all such matters in a written form.

Deafness had been a great advantage to him in telegraphy. He could hear the loud ticking of the instruments infallibly but did not hear the other distracting noises.

At one time he had been elected to a luncheon club where dinners were always given with many speeches. At first he regretted not being able to hear them. Later, they printed the accompany them they did. The Edisons returned to Newark to occupy an eight-room house he had purchased at 97 Wright Street.

At the time he had been perfecting the transmission of the alphabet over the wires and, at the same time, was working on 46 other inventions. Working with two telegraphers, Ed Johnson and Patrick Delaney, each night on long distance wires between New York City and a town in the Carolinas, the method was perfected enough to try it in England.

An Englishman, George Little, had developed a system of automatic telegraphy. Using a paper tape, perforations were made in it corresponding to the Morse code. In running it through a transmitting machine rapidly, the ribbon would pass over a cylinder and an electrical contact was made by a metallic pen that dropped into the holes as they passed by, thereby transmitting signals. The signals were received on an ink-writing recorder or on a kind of typewriter. It worked well on the short lines but failed on long ones.

General W. T. Palmer and his New York associates had acquired the Little system but soon found it was imperfect—the wire was sluggish and the equipment needed improvement. Edward H. Johnson left a Colorado railroad building job to assist Edison when the latter agreed to assume the task of improvement for the Automatic Telegraph Company. Edison progressed to a point that 1,000 words a minute were transmitted and received between New York and Washington, D.C., and 3,500 words a minute to Philadelphia. Manual key transmission rarely exceeded 40 or 50 words a minute.

By using a shunt around the receiver the auto-induction caused a momentary delay in each signal, giving it a sharp definition so the signals would not run together in hopeless confusion as before, thus permitting very high speeds.

It was Edison's idea to develop an automatic that would print the message received, in Roman letters. The company, now encouraged with his development of the automatic equipment, had rented a large and well-equipped shop for him in Newark. In a test between New York and Philadelphia he was able to send 3,000 words in one minute, receiving and recording them in Roman type. This meant that the message thus received could be torn off and delivered, saving the expense of having a clerk translate a dot and dash message into

ELISHA GRAY, working independently of Alexander Graham Bell, filed in the Patent Office a preliminary statement (caveat) outlining the invention of an instrument that transmitted the human voice, on the same day Bell did. Bell won the patent priority. 1890. Library of Congress.

GLASS BLOWERS in the Edison Lamp Works at Menlo Park in late 1880. This was the same building in which Edison's electric pens had been made and was used for manufacturing lamps until April, 1882, when the manufacturing was moved to larger quarters at Harrison, New Jersey, to take care of the great demand for lamps. Edison National Historic Site.

words and then write it out.

In an effort to introduce Edison's successful automatic system in England, Colonel George E. Gouraud arranged for a demonstration on a wire between Liverpool and London. Though Tom's first child, Marion, had been born on February 18, 1873, he left for England on April 29 with his assistant Jack Wright on the steamer *Java*. After they overcame some technical difficulties the test was quite successful.

The British authorities asked him if the system could work on submarine cables. Since his response was affirmative a test was arranged. No cable was available just then so arrangements were made to use 2,200 miles of coiled cable intended for a line to Brazil that was stored in tanks of water. Once Tom had his apparatus set up he sent a single dot to get an idea of the amount of distortion to expect. It appeared on the receiver as a line 27 feet long. He said afterward, "If I ever had any conceit, it vanished from my boots up!"

Two weeks' work on the cable produced two words a minute which was one-seventh of the speed guaranteed once the cable was laid. The plan was abandoned and Edison returned to the United States late in June. What he did not learn until later "was that a coiled cable, owing to induction, was infinitely worse than when laid out straight, and that my speed was as good as, if not better than, the regular system; but no one told me this."

He had been working on the multiple transmission of telegraphic messages—duplex telegraphy it was called. Joseph Stearns had invented a system of sending two messages in opposite directions at the same time on a single wire. In April, 1873, Edison filed a patent application on a plan to send two messages at the same time and in the same direction on a single wire. This was called the diplex.

Edison had returned to a country undergoing the agony of a Great Depression. A panic was in progress, growing unemployment adding its pressure. Edison had left his business in a precarious state. His reserve funds spent, his credit maintained by postponing payments, his property taxes unpaid, and a court case pending against him, he was in a precarious predicament. He was about to lose all. An amicable agreement with a friendly sheriff delayed action until he could get back on his feet. He was ready to do anything that would bring in enough money to prevent disaster.

Tom applied himself in developing several refinements in the field of telegraphy. William Orton, president of Western Union, asked Edison why four messages could not be sent over the wire instead of two. Agreeing to try it if he was loaned eight operators and the wires to experiment on, he dropped all his other work to speed results. This caused him to neglect his business which added to its financial straits.

Early in the summer of 1874 he had been working on a chalk relay for Jay Gould's telegraph network, the Atlantic and Pacific. Gould had given Tom $10,000 on account and this enabled him to lift a mortgage on his property. Western Union had given no advances, yet he continued to work on the quadruplex telegraph.

The problem was all absorbing and, as he said, "It required peculiar effort of the mind, such as the imagining of eight different things moving simultaneously on a mental plane without anything to demonstrate their efficiency."

During the summer of 1874 Edison was ready to give a demonstration of the quadruplex before a Western Union board meeting. Having selected the best operators in New York for the occasion, and realizing that a bad storm could seriously interfere with transmission and reception, he arranged with them to use their imaginations since they were sending old messages. As he had anticipated, there was a bad storm near Albany, but the operators handled the situation masterfully. Though the demonstration was a success Orton avoided closing the deal with the financially embarrassed Edison.

The principle of the Edison Quadruplex is that of working over a line with two electric currents from each end that differ from each other in strength or nature, so they will affect only those instruments adapted to respond to just such currents and no others; and by so arranging the receiving apparatus as not to be affected by the currents transmitted from its own end of the line. Four sending and four receiving operators are kept busy at each end—eight in all. It is estimated that the Edison Quadruplex has saved $15 to $20 million in line construction in America. It was considered to be the most important contribution to telegraphy since its origin by Morse.

The day following the demonstration The New York *Times* came out with a full account. Orton came through with $5,000 in part payment, then abruptly left on an extended trip. Tom immediately used it all to pay his annoying creditors. This left him short of funds with which to continue his experimentation.

Soon afterward, General T. T. Eckert, general superintendent of Western Union, called upon Tom. Eckert advised him he would never receive another cent from Orton, but that he knew of a place the quadruplex could be sold. Eckert made an appointment to bring Jay Gould to the 10-12 Ward Street shop for a demonstration. The day following the demonstration Eckert took him to Gould's house. Gould immediately asked him how much he wanted. He already knew that Tom had a partnership agreement with a chief electrician of Western Union—this chief electrician, George B. Prescott, was no inventor but wanted only the glory of being a coinventor in return for having used his influence in Edison's behalf — that would not hinder any transaction.

Tom said, "Make me an offer." Gould replied, "I will give you $30,000." Tom responded with, "I will sell any interest I may have for that money." The next morning in the office of Gould's lawyers he received a check for the amount agreed upon. In delivering it to Tom, Gould remarked that he was giving him his steamboat the *Plymouth Rock* as he had just sold it for that amount.

Gould never missed an opportunity of mak-

ing a dollar. Learning of the success of Edison's automatic telegraph—Gould had visions of obtaining control of Western Union—he made an offer to purchase the Automatic Telegraph Company in exchange for $4 million dollars worth of Atlantic & Pacific stock. Edison and his associates agreed to the offer. In the end Edison, along with the others, was swindled out of his share by Gould. Three years of hard work, $250,000 in securities and the promised position of chief electrician for the new amalgamated company went down the drain. Though Edison was through with Gould by the summer of 1875 he bore him no malice and held no grudge "because he was so able in his line."

Tom liked diversions. Relief from the pressure of an overwhelming problem was obtained temporarily by diverting his attention to another one equally absorbing. D. N. Craig, one of the organizers of the Associated Press, brought in a Mr. Sholes from Milwaukee with a wooden model of a machine he called a typewriter. Sholes was running into difficulties and wanted Tom to perfect it. The letters tended to wander out of line and a letter might be one-sixteenth above another. Tom worked on it "till the machine gave fair results." Sholes hoped to see it used for all business letters but died before that occured. The typewriter Edison worked on for Sholes is now known as the Remington.

With five shops and all of his experimenting to do Tom was excessively busy. He had invented a messenger call box system that he was putting into use by organizing a company called the Domestic Telegraph Company. The

**MENLO PARK MACHINE SHOP CREW** pauses long enough to be photographed. 1880. Three men near tree, left to right: William Mills, Ludwig Boehm, George Dean. John Kreusi is in front of closed door; William S. Andrews stands to his right. Others unidentified. Edison National Historic Site.

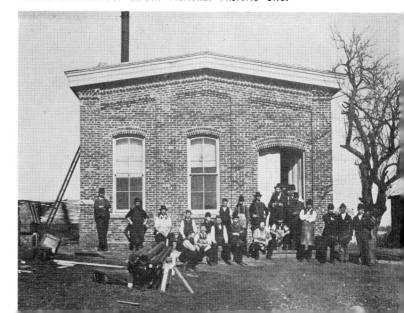

system provided an emergency call service as a protection against burglary, fire or an acute illness. Obtaining subscribers was quite difficult. Six men had failed to sell the service on a house-to-house canvass but a seventh obtained 200 in a month, insuring success. This Edison could not understand though he did understand why the Atlantic and Pacific Company bought it out.

About this time he developed what we know today as paraffin paper and which has since seen universal use on bread, candies, chocolate and chewing gum.

He relates that, "Toward the latter part of 1875, in the Newark shop I invented a device for multiplying copies of letters, which I sold to Mr. A. B. Dick, of Chicago, and in the years since had been introduced universally throughout the world. It is called the mimeograph . . ." The device then called the Edison Electric Pen was operated by two wet cell batteries that caused a pointed pencil-like stylus to rapidly puncture a sheet of paper with numerous small holes, filling such holes with a semi-fluid ink, and pressing this same upon the surface to be printed. Any letters or records so perforated had the advantage that many copies could be made from them. Some 60,000 were sold for rapid copying, the pens selling for eight dollars, the roller for three dollars and the battery for five dollars.

In a moment of realization and logic he concluded that the vexations of business and manufacturing were an intrusion on his investigative research. If he was to progress in the manner he wished, he must divorce himself from the aggravations of those endeavors.

**STAR BOARDERS** on the porch of the Jordan boarding house, about 1879. Left to right: Dr. A. E. Haid, Mrs. Sarah Jordan, Laura Jordan, Major McLaughlin, S. L. Griffin, Mrs. S. Van Cleve, Miss Van Cleve, Francis R. Upton, Thomas A. Edison, Alice Stillwell (in window), Charles Batchelor, John W. Lawson, Francis Jehl. Edison National Historic Site.

Chapter Six

# Move To Menlo

If inventing was his business there must be a better place in which to do it, Edison reasoned. He had some ideas as to a location but was so occupied with a phenomena he had discovered—he called it etheric force—that he sent for his father to survey the area around Newark for a site that could be used for an experimental laboratory. Sam arrived on November 1, 1875, and promptly began the task assigned.

Sam finally concluded that the best site was a hilltop near the tiny village of Menlo Park, New Jersey, a few miles below Elizabeth and some 25 miles southwest of New York. This secluded area gave Tommy—as Sam called his son—protection from the manufacturing interests in Newark.

Utilizing his father's considerable experience in the lumber business, Tom put him to use by having him superintend the construction of a two-story wooden structure 28 x 100 feet. The ground floor housed his equipment and the second floor his chemical laboratory. Soon afterward it was followed by a machine shop, carpentry shop, office and library, and a few smaller buildings. Here he had the seclusion he needed, yet he was within a short distance of the contacts and supplies so necessary to success.

When he moved from Newark into his new laboratory he sold all of his machinery. He had given his landlord, from whom he rented the top floor of a padlock factory, a month's rent and notice that he was to move. After he had vacated the premises and returned the keys he was served a legal notice that he owed nine months' rent, there being a law that made a month-to-month renter liable for a full year's rent. The unjustness of the law made him more certain that leaving Newark for a community with different standards was a wise decision.

The tiny hamlet of Menlo Park boasted of seven houses. Its main street was Christie Street and led from the Edison laboratory to the main highway that ran between New York City and Philadelphia. A short distance from the laboratory was Mrs. Jordan's boarding house which became famous as the first residence to be lighted by electricity. It was there that most of Edison's employees lived and boarded. For five or six dollars a week an individual was provided with a room furnished with a bureau, bed, commode with wash bowl and pitcher, and illuminated with a candle or a kerosene lamp. There was plenty of food with each meal, the noon-day lunch consisting of soup, potatoes, meat and pies for which she was famous. Down the street near the railway station an old Scotchman named Davis kept a small saloon.

WILLIAM ORTON became president of the Western Union Telegraph Company aftter the Civil War. In 1873 he permitted Edison to use Western Union facilities for research on the duplex and quadruplex provided any such inventions would be sold to the company. Western Union Telegraph Co.

GENERAL T. T. ECKERT, while General Superintendent of the Western Union in 1875, when Orton failed to purchase Edison's new quadruplex, arranged a meeting between Jay Gould and Edison. Gould paid Edison $30,000 for the quadruplex. Eckert became president of Gould's Atlantic & Pacific Telegraph Company. Western Union Telegraph Company.

The upper floor of Edison's laboratory was used for the more important experiments such as the incandescent lamp. The side walls were lined with shelves filled with thousands of bottles of chemicals. Several long tables held scientific and chemical apparatus of those times. Books and models lay here and there. At the far end of the room was a pipe organ and near it stood a large glass case holding precious metals and rare chemicals.

The main floor had a testing table resting on two large pillars of bricks that ran deep into the ground to eliminate vibrations when special instruments were used upon it. Nearby was the chemical laboratory.

The machine shop was next door. Built of brick, it had a boiler and engine room at one end. The main shop contained boring and drilling machines, planing machines, light and heavy lathes and every type of tool available. John Kruesi was in charge of it, assisted by John Ott. Tom usually had three or four assistants selected for physical endurance, compatibility and skill.

Between the machine shop and the laboratory was a small wooden building used as a carpentry shop by Tom Logan. Prior to the incandescent lamp all illumination was obtained from gasoline vapor which was used for glass blowing also.

At the edge of his property was a small building containing a battery of coal oil lamps whose wicks were turned up to produce the maximum of soot. Alfred Swanson, the night watchman, would collect this soot. After being weighed out in small portions it was pressed into small buttons, packed between layers of cotton, and shipped to Sigmund Bergmann in New York for use in the construction of telephone transmitters.

Back in 1861, Johann Philipp Reis, a German professor, had invented a kind of telephone that could operate but a few seconds before it went out of adjustment. William Orton in July, 1875, had provided Edison with a translation of a description of the equipment which stimulated him to experiment with the fault in it.

Alexander Graham Bell, having observed the Reis apparatus while filing a patent on a multiple telegraph he had worked on, went home to experiment on transmitting the human voice.

Then in November, 1875, Tom observed a new phenomenon—a spark that sprang from a magnet. It was unusual in that the spark could be obtained by touching any metallic part of the magnet or when the wire was turned around itself. This unknown force had no polarity nor had it respect for insulation. Delighted with this discovery, he called it an "etheric force." His demonstration of it before the American Institute created much excitement.

In the December, 1875, *Operator,* Edison wrote: "The cumbersome appliances of transmitting ordinary electricity such as telegraph poles, insulating knobs, cables, sheathings and so on, may be left out of the problem of quick and cheap telegraphic transmission; and a great saving of time and labor accomplished."

About this time (February 14, 1876) Bell applied for his patent for the magneto telephone. This was too much for Tom. He stopped his experiments on etheric force and returned to his telephone experiments. By doing so he lost the opportunity of discovering the wireless, and he already had passed up the opportunity of being named the inventor of the telephone.

He had filed a caveat at the patent office (January 14, 1876) a month ahead of Bell, describing a device for analyzing sound waves. It consisted of a hollow metal tube with two electromagnets against the diaphragmlike end inside of which was fitted another metal tube. In experimenting with it later he learned that one tube could be used successfully as a receiver and the other as a transmitter.

Bell's telephone had limited usefulness because of its faintness and since it served both as a transmitter and a receiver. By strenuous

**GEORGE BERNARD SHAW,** while young and poor (1878), demonstrated the operation of the telephone for the Edison Telephone Company in London. Edison National Historic Site.

**EDISON CARBON TRANSMITTER AND CHALK RECEIVER.** Edison's use of carbon was such a vast improvement it enabled his transmitter to displace Bell's magnetic transmitter. The chalk receiver was developed for use by the Edison Telephone Company of Great Britain where it was quite successful in its competition with Bell's instrument. Edison National Historic Site.

**AN EARLY EDISON CARBON TELEPHONE.** Bell's first telephone was impractical. The instrument was both transmitter and receiver and very weak. In 1877 Edison added his carbon transmitter and an induction coil so his transmitter would have a range far beyond the few miles of Bell's. Edison National Historic Site.

**THE QUADRUPLEX TELEGRAPH REPEATER** was totally an Edison invention. George B. Prescott, Western Union's chief engineer, received a half interest in the invention for which Edison received the attention of Orton. Smithsonian Institution.

UNITED STATES PATENT OFFICE.

THOMAS A. EDISON, OF NEWARK, NEW JERSEY, ASSIGNOR OF ONE-HALF HIS RIGHT TO GEORGE B. PRESCOTT.

IMPROVEMENT IN QUADRUPLEX-TELEGRAPH REPEATERS.

Specification forming part of Letters Patent No. 209,241, dated October 22, 1878; application filed March 23, 1875.

CASE No. 113.

*To all whom it may concern:*

Be it known that I, THOMAS A. EDISON, of Newark, in the county of Essex and State of New Jersey, have invented an Improvement in Quadruplex Telegraphs, of which the following is a specification:

The object of this invention is to repeat from one quadruplex circuit into another quadruplex circuit.

In my present invention I make use of two quadruplex circuits, in which the signals are made by rise and fall of tension in one relay-magnet, and by change of polarity in the other relay-magnet, which is polarized. The modes of connecting and operating have been fully set forth in applications heretofore made by me.

The present improvement relates to the connections from one quadruplex telegraph to another, whereby the circuits work into and operate each other, so that the messages are repeated automatically in one circuit by the receiving-instrument of the other circuit, instead of the finger-key being operated by hand.

The entire apparatus and connections for repeating, as aforesaid, are shown in the diagram, which, although it appears complicated, is very simple. One line, L, comes, for instance, from New York to one set of instruments at an intermediate station—say Buffalo—and the other line, L, extends to the distant instruments—say at Chicago—in the other direction.

The keys and instruments are duplicated and exactly the same, only there are two distinct sets of instruments.

Suppose that a message over the wire L from New York acts by rise and fall of tension in the relay-magnet M, and that this message is repeated into the sounder or receiving-instrument g'. If the switch 42 in the local circuit of the battery f' is closed, the message goes no farther; but if the switch 44 is open the circuit of the battery f' extends to the electro-magnet, the switch of the key a being open. Thereby the message received at M on one line is repeated by c and K into the next

line. So, in like manner, the message received from New York in the differential magnet D M and repeated in the sounder s will go no farther if the switch 42 is closed; but if the switch 42 is open the message will be repeated to Chicago at the key b by the magnet d and key R K, that reverses the circuit in the same manner as if the finger-key b were operated.

Of course, by opening the switch 41 the message coming over the line L from Chicago and received in M will be repeated to New York, and the same thing will occur in relation to the message received in D M from Chicago if the switch 43 is closed. Thus one or more messages may be automatically repeated in long lines without interfering with the working of the other portions of the quadruplex instruments in either direction from the intermediate station.

In an application for Letters Patent filed by me September 4, 1874, Case 99, circuit-preserving keys for changing the polarity of the current and for increasing or decreasing the electric tension, like those shown in this application, and instruments for responding to the pulsations sent by these keys are shown. I therefore do not herein lay any claim to the same.

What I claim is—

1. In combination with two main-line circuits, each capable of quadruplex operation, the repeating-magnets, local circuits, switches, and connections, arranged substantially as set forth, so that either message may be repeated independently of other messages, substantially as set forth.

2. The combination, with the receiving-sounders in one line, of repeating-instruments, local circuits and switches, and transmitting-instruments in the other line, arranged and operating substantially as and for the purposes set forth.

Signed by me this 24th day of February, A. D. 1875.

THOMAS A. EDISON.

Witnesses:
GEO. T. PINCKNEY,
GEO. D. WALKER.

shouting a man could be heard over the wire a distance of two miles. Tom recognized its commercial limitations so proceeded to eliminate the obvious deficiencies.

Orton, learning of Edison's attempts at improvement, approached him with a request that he make the instrument commercially usable. He offered him $150 a week for five years toward his expenses in return for a first claim on any of his inventions. Edison signed the agreement prepared by the Western Union's counsel Grosvenor P. Lowrey. One month later he filed a patent application for a separate transmitter.

Using a fatiguing thoroughness in his search for a solution he literlly searched for "a needle in a haystack," removing a straw at a time. The spring and summer of 1877 were occupied by a continuous series of telephone experiments in a search for a perfect transmitter.

One of the first things he had done was to use a separate apparatus for transmitting and another for receiving. He had attacked the problem of increasing the telephone's volume. Having tried a great variety of substances against the diaphragm of the transmitter— drops of water, moistened sponges, paper, felt, graphite, white Arkansas oilstone, then carbon collected from the chimneys of coal oil lamps and pressed into a small button—he discovered that a carbon button in contact with a vibrating diaphragm created impulses in the receiving magnet and, in turn, caused its diaphragm to vibrate and reproduce the sounds transmitted from the transmitter. Where Bell's telephone generated extremely weak impulses, Edison's electrical impulses were powerful.

During 1878—August 27—he applied for a telephone transmitter patent to cover his use of carbon in it (Patent No. 474,230), thus creating the first microphone.

Now that he had perfected the carbon transmitter, tests were made between New York, Philadelphia and Washington, with Orton, Vanderbilt and directors of the Western Union taking part. Bell's instrument was useless in attempts at conversation between New York and Newark. Edison's carbon transmitter was successful.

Orton asked Edison how much he wanted for it. Tom, having $25,000 in his mind, asked Orton to make an offer. Orton promptly responded with an offer of $100,000 to which Tom replied, "All right, it is yours on one condition, and that is that you do not pay it all at once,

DRAPER ASTRONOMICAL EXPEDITION in Rawlins, Wyoming, July 1878. Edison's tasimeter protrudes from the small coop in the center. Left to right: Professor George F. Barker, University of Pennsylvania; Robert M. Galbraith, master mechanic, Union Pacific Railroad; Henry Morton, president, Stevens Institute; Mr. Bloomfield; Mr. Meyers; D. H. Talbot, Sioux City; M. F. Rae; Marshall Fox, New York **Herald** correspondent; James C. Watson; Mrs. A. H. Watson; Mrs. Henry Draper; Dr. Henry Draper, Albany Observatory; Thomas A. Edison; J. Norman Lockyer, editor, **Nature** (London). July, 1878. Edison National Historic Site.

but pay me at the rate of $6,000 a year for 17 years—the life of the patent." Orton accepted the deal while Edison had protected himself and his family by avoiding 17 years of worry; he recognized his great fault of disregarding financial security through indiscriminate spending of his reserve savings on experimentation.

He obtained some relief from all of his telephone experimentation by dropping back to advanced ideas in the development of his new automatic telegraph repeater. On July 18, 1877, while trying out some revolving paper discs on the Western Union lines, an excessive amount of current was used on the motor, causing his discs to spin so rapidly the metal point fairly skimmed in and out of the indentations in the paper. As a result, sound became audible.

In his notebook he wrote: "Just tried experiment with a diaphragm having an embossed point and held against parafin paper moving rapidly. The speaking vibrations are indented nicely and there is no doubt that I shall be able to store up and reproduce automatically at any future time the human voice perfectly."

A few days before December 6 he gave "Honest" John Kruesi a sketch from which he turned out a special metal cylinder and shaft—a model of the first talking machine. The cylinder, covered with tinfoil, after a few adjustments, was hand turned as a blunt pin played over its surface. Speaking into a mouthpiece attached to a diaphragm and a blunt pin, Tom recited a nursery favorite, "Mary had a little lamb."

To everyone's consternation, even Edison's,

"TEXAS JACK," known at home as John Burwell Omohundro —an expert pistol shot—was one of the Wyoming "good guys." An admirer of Edison's, he greeted him on his arrival in Rawlins. An 1876 sketch. Denver Public Library Western Collection.

TEXAS JACK.

**ORIGINAL TIN FOIL PHONOGRAPH INVENTED BY THOMAS A. EDISON.** The grooved cylinder was covered with tin foil and turned by hand against a needle or stylus that was attached to a diaphragm on each side. Edison's first words shouted into the diaphragm were:

Mary had a little lamb,
Its fleece was white as snow,
And everywhere that Mary went
The lamb was sure to go.

Rewinding the shaft to its original position, Edison adjusted the other diaphragm, then turned the crank again. From the phonograph came the thin voice of Edison in fine reproduction, to the amazement of his staff. Edison National Historic Site.

**LETTER WRITTEN TO J. U. MACKENZIE,** the man who taught Edison telegraphy. Edison National Historic Site.

the cylinder played back the words just spoken into the mouthpiece when it was placed at the starting point and the crank was turned.

Edward H. Johnson, an associate of Edison's, while on a lecture tour that summer of 1877, had used a good part of each lecture describing a device of Edison's that would register speech vibrations from a needle and diaphragm on a continuous strip of paper which in turn, could be repeated over the telephone as a kind of automatic telephone.

One newspaper referred to it as a *talking machine* which intensified the interest in Johnson's lectures and drew large crowds. This was the first time Edison realized he had a talking machine and it was within 24 hours after this that he devised, made and operated his first phonograph.

Edison tells of it in this fashion:

"I discovered the principle by the merest accident. I was singing to the mouthpiece of a telephone, when the vibrations of the voice sent the fine steel point into my finger. That set me thinking. If I could record the actions of the point and send the point over the same surface afterward, I saw no reason why the thing would not talk. I tried the experiment first on a strip of telegraph paper and found that the point made an alphabet. I shouted the words 'Halloo! Halloo!' into the mouthpiece, ran the paper back over the steel point, and heard a faint 'Halloo! Halloo!' in return. I determined to make a machine that would work accurately, and gave my assistants instructions, telling them what I discovered. They laughed at me. That's the whole story. The phonograph is the result of pricking a finger."

A year earlier he had taken out a patent for "a method of recording ordinary telegraphic signals, by a chisel-shaped stylus, indenting a sheet of paper, enveloping a cylinder or plate along the groove cut in the surface of the latter." The purpose of the indented marks was to use them for automatic transmission over another telegraph wire.

One day General Benjamin F. Butler, while examining one of Edison's telephones, remarked, "Now Edison, you must make something to record these sounds." Soon afterward Edison was at the Smithsonian Institution examining an instrument used to outline sound waves, which caused him to say, "Wise men,

**FRONT STREET, RAWLINS, WYOMING.** Edison stayed in Rawlins with the Draper Astronomical Expedition, which he accompanied, to observe the solar eclipse July 29, 1878. 1883. From the Brimmer Collection, Western History Research Center, University of Wyoming Library.

these were, not to see that they could put a hard point and a piece of tinfoil in front of it, and there is the phonograph."

The newly invented talking machine created excitement all over the world. Everyone wanted to hear it and where it was used for exhibition purposes huge crowds would gather. The tin-foil recordings astonished everyone the first time they were heard. Edison had been astonished the first time he had heard it play, primarily because it had reproduced so perfectly. He had a built-in fear "of things that worked the first time."

To protect the original phonograph he expected to get a patent on every kind of phonograph he could think of—probably a dozen in all. He considered one in ten of his patents of real practical value, the others having been taken out as a protection against stealing his main idea. With nothing in the Patent Office files resembling or approaching his invention and no "reference" or "interference" cited or registered, he was granted a patent February 19, 1878.

Soon after this he proclaimed that a European invention developed to provide instantaneous photographs might take pictures every second of Henry Ward Beecher while his sermon was taken down on tin-foil, then both could be reproduced together and shown in the parlor at home — an 1878 prediction of the sound movie.

**INVENTION OF A SYSTEM.** Not just a lamp and a dynamo, but an entire system of distributing electric current for heat, light and power had been invented by Edison. Edison National Historic Site.

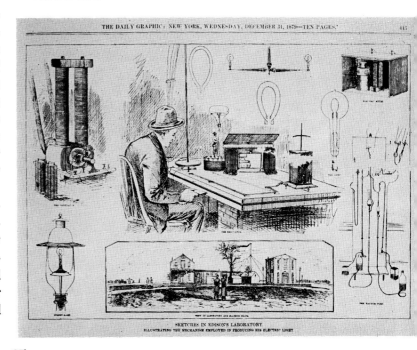

67

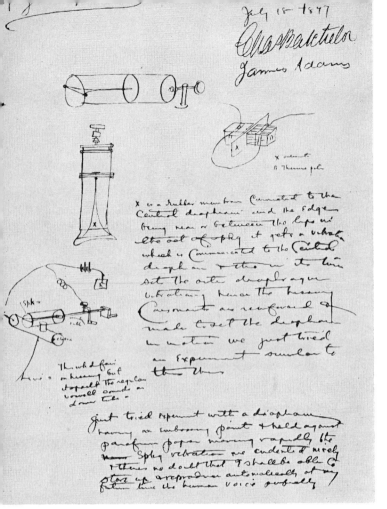

**SKETCH** relating to the telephone. The notation at the bottom of the sketch made on July 18, 1877, is thought to be the first indication Edison did any experiment on the phonograph. Edison National Historic Site.

**TIN FOIL PHONOGRAPH SKETCH** made by Edison on November 29, 1877, is presumed to be that used by John Kruesi in constructing the first model completed and tested December 6, 1877. Edison National Historic Site.

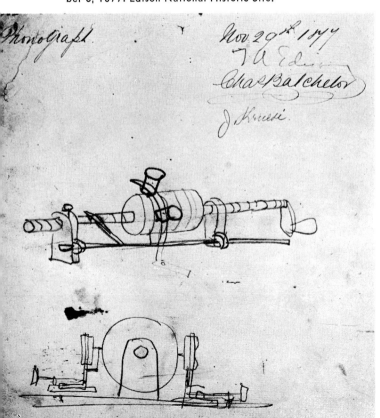

On April 18, 1878, he was asked to demonstrate his phonograph before the National Academy of Sciences in Washington, D. C. Dressed in a new checkered suit and accompanied by Charles Batchelor, he no more than stepped off the train when news correspondent Uriah Painter met him with an invitation from James G. Blaine's niece, Gail Hamilton, asking him and Batchelor to her apartment to demonstrate the phonograph to prominent Congressmen and members of the diplomatic corps, then later at the White House to President Hayes.

After breakfasting at Willard's Hotel, they visited Joseph Henry, secretary of the Smithsonian Institution, demonstrating the machine for him in his parlor. That afternoon they made their presentation before the Academy and were followed by Professor George F. Barker of the University of Pennsylvania, who gave a paper on Edison's accomplishments in perfecting a carbon telephone transmitter capable of messages over a distance of 140 miles. Near midnight President Hayes received Edison and it was 3 a.m. before he left the White House.

Edison had become a mythical figure, almost a mystic, to the general public. Writers and cartoonists had augmented this feeling, the publicity creating great jealousies among inventors. In order to handle the vast correspondence resulting from his renown, Edison added Stockton L. Griffin, chief of Western Union's eastern wires, to his staff.

It was not Edison's nature to direct his interest and energy toward one thing at a time. Though deeply immersed in a particular problem, he might be diverted temporarily by a phenomena that crossed his path that he would not permit to escape without minute examination. While working on the carbon transmitter he had discovered that slight increases in pressure on carbon decreased its resistance to the flow of electric current. And he observed that hard rubber would expand if heat was applied to it. The thought came to him that by combining the two he could devise an instrument that could measure heat in minute degrees. The final result was a carbon button placed between two platinum plates in contact with a hard rubber rod, forming an electric circuit in which was a battery and a galvanometer. When the hard rubber was exposed to heat it would expand against the carbon button producing a variation in resistance that would cause the galvanometer needle to register. This instrument, called a tasimeter, he believed would register heat variations down to one-millionth of a degree Fahrenheit.

It was late in the spring of 1878 and he was not feeling very well. Long work hours and no vacation for seven years had taken their toll. Badly in need of a change and relaxation, he accepted Professor George F. Barker's invitation to accompany the Henry Draper Astronomical Expedition to Rawlins. Wyoming, in time to observe a total eclipse of the sun July 29, 1878.

Rawlins had been selected as the site for witnessing the solar eclipse because it was the highest town near the Continental Divide that offered clear and sunny weather. Its altitude was 6,755 feet. In 1874, Rawlins had received some attention by having provided a carload of pigment from its Red Paint mines for painting the Brooklyn Bridge.

The Draper party Edison joined had been provided with a special car for its trip over the Union Pacific Railroad. Dr. Draper, who was a

**PAPER FILAMENTS WERE CARBONIZED BY BAKING.** The "Wizard of Menlo Park" tried everything from paper to human hair in his search for a better lamp filament. Edison National Historic Site.

**THE FIRST SUCCESSFUL INCANDESCENT LAMP** was invented by Edison on October 19, 1879. Its filament was a carbonized cotton sewing thread—as in this replica—that burned for 40 hours. Edison National Historic Site.

scientist specializing in celestial photography at the Albany Observatory, was accompanied by his wife. Dr. Barker of Philadelphia, Professor Morton of Hoboken, Theodore Whitney of St. Augustine, Florida, and Marshall Fox, star reporter for the New York *Herald,* completed the party.

Soon after their arrival at Rawlins their party heard the latest story going the rounds. It seems that several weeks earlier, Dutch Charlie Burris and Big Nose George Parrot had attempted to derail the westbound Union Pacific pay car nearby. In their get-away they had killed Tip Vincent and Ed Widowfield for which they were being sought by the law.

The town's only hotel was small but it accommodated everyone by doubling up its guests. Edison's roommate was the reporter, Marshall Fox.

Tired from travel, both were in bed and asleep when they were suddenly awakened by a thundering knock on their door. Edison recalled, "Upon opening the door, a tall, handsome man with flowing hair, dressed in western style, entered the room. His eyes were bloodshot, and he was somewhat inebriated. He introduced himself as 'Texas Jack'—John B. Omohundro— and said he wanted to see Edison as he had read about me in the newspapers.''

The two roommates were quite shaken with all this, and more so when the landlord came in to ask Jack to be quiet and was thrown unceremoniously into the hall. As if he had not been interrupted, Jack went on to tell them he had been away hunting and felt just fine. Explaining that he was the best pistol shot in the West, having taught Doc Carver how to shoot, he pointed to a weather vane on the freight

**THOMAS A. EDISON SITS FOR PHOTOGRAPHER MATHEW B. BRADY.** Brady made this photograph April 18, 1878, while young Edison was in Washington to demonstrate his tin foil phonograph to President Rutherford B. Hayes at the White House and before the National Academy of Sciences meeting. Edison National Historic Site.

THE DAILY GRAPHIC

An Illustrated Evening Newspaper.

39 & 41 Park Place

VOL. XXI.    All the News, Four Editions Daily.    NEW YORK, SATURDAY, JANUARY 3, 1880.    $12 Per Year in Advance. Single Copies, Five Cents.

EDISON AND HIS ELECTRIC LIGHT
SCENES AT MENLO PARK ON NEW YEAR'S EVE.

**PUBLICITY ON THE FIRST PUBLIC DEMONSTRATION.** About 3,000 people visited Menlo Park on New Year's Eve of 1880 to see the laboratories and village streets illuminated by a new light source. New York Public Library.

depot, suddenly whipped out a Colt revolver and hit the vane by firing through the window.

This was enough to awaken everyone. The hotel soon buzzed with activity, all rushing in to see who had been killed. Jack finally left the room when Edison told him he was tired and would see him in the morning. More than slightly upset, neither Tom nor Fox slept the rest of that night. The next day they were set at ease when told that Jack was not one of the bad men that area amply supplied.

That day Edison introduced himself to the manager of the Western Union office, Nute

Craig. When Craig learned of Edison's former association with Western Union, he responded to Edison's request for office space for Dr. Draper and himself by offering to put a table in the telegraph office for them.

Edison needed some space to put a few pieces of equipment so Craig obtained consent of the owner of a house next door to use it any way Edison saw fit, the family occupying it having gone East. Immediately Edison set up a laboratory in the kitchen, for he had been working with his experiments on the incandescent lamp.

Craig, at Edison's request, had the chicken-coop roof removed and his tasimeter installed with a four-inch telescope attached to it. Professor S. P. Langley of Allegheny University, who originally had suggested the microtasimeter to Edison, had invited him to measure the heat of the stellar spectra with it. The tasimeter's value was its ability to detect and measure the smallest temperature variation of any object it was directed at. The instrument had been completed just two days before Edison had left for the West. By use of the telescope an image of the star Arcturus was cast upon the tasimeter's rubber rod and five successful readings were made denoting the heat of the star.

Edison's kitchen laboratory window offered a fine view of Wyoming hills on which could be seen an abundance of antelope. Feeling the urge to shoot an antelope, he asked Craig to buy him a Winchester sporting rifle. In a target practice session in which Edison twice missed a tin can at 50 yards, Craig put a bullet dead center at his first try. After watching Edison's continued lack of success, he returned to his office. Edison returned later to display a can full of holes. For the two following mornings he hunted antelope unsuccessfully.

One day some of the party headed 13 miles westward to Separation where the government astronomers had prepared an observation point on the crest of the Continental Divide. Having been told by the telegraph operator there were plenty of jackrabbits around, Fox and Edison had brought their Winchesters with them. Spying some jackrabbits—the residents called them narrow-gauge mules—in the clear, Edison advanced to within 100 feet and fired, with no effect. Moving to a ten-foot distance he fired again, with no effect. Closer observation revealed it was a stuffed rabbit. An interested crowd at the station had been watching the daring hunt. Swearing the stationmen to silence, they "baited" Professor Newcomb and several

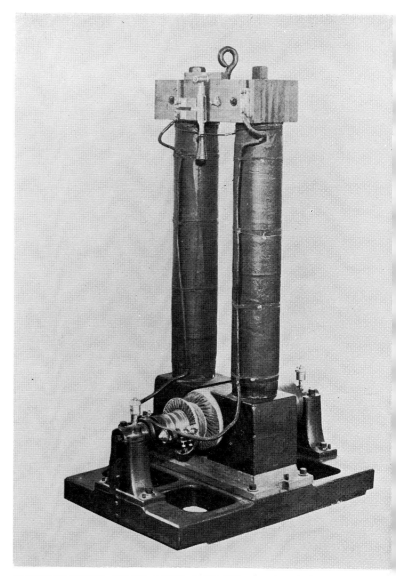

"LONG-WAISTED MARY ANN" DYNAMO developed by Edison in 1879. Its 90 per cent efficiency was double that of previous dynamos. Edison National Historic Site.

others, everyone enjoying the fun.

The day of the eclipse, July 29, was stormy. Encompassing difficulty in his frail hencoop, the vibration from the wind causing the tasimeter to require continuous adjustment, Edison stabilized the fragile building with planks as props. Within one minute of the total eclipse he managed to obtain a reading that indicated 15 times more heat than the star Arcturus registered the night before. He had determined that the corona's heat was much greater than that of some of the fixed stars and that his tasimeter was much too sensitive for the task at hand.

Following the eclipse, Edison, Professor Barker, Major Thomas T. Thornburgh with several of his soldiers and a few railroad officials went hunting and fishing 100 miles south into the

Ute country. Several months later Major Thornburgh and 30 soldiers were ambushed and killed near a spot on which the Edison hunting party had previously camped.

Swarthy, six-foot Tom Sun, a well-known guide, had led Edison and his friends on the expedition, supplying all of the equipment. Craig, in forwarding a telegram to Edison then several days south of Rawlins, asked Sun's partner Sam Morgan to take it to him. Asked later by Craig if the party had been hard to find, Morgan said, "No, it was easy. I can track Edison anywhere by the tobacco juice on the grass."

When the hunting party returned to Rawlins, Craig saw them unload a deer with a fine rack of antlers. When he asked who shot it, Edison said he had. In disbelief Craig asked Tom Sun later, and Tom supported Edison's statement, adding that the buck had been killed by one shot just back of the shoulder.

Wyoming pioneers have handed down a story that Edison, while fishing at Battle Lake that August, 1878, became interested in the fiber of his bamboo fishing pole, later using it in a test for the filament of his incandescent lamp.

Thomas Edison never liked to look back. He said that spilt milk didn't interest him for he had spilt a lot of it and felt it for a few days but quickly forgot it. 1881. Edison National Historic Site.

Edison had derived a great deal of good from the trip up to that point. Not only had he obtained a much needed rest and change but he had the stimulus of viewing vast areas of frontier that could benefit from the use of electricity. Observing many places where grain was hauled as far as 200 miles by horse and wagon because rail transportation was unavailable, he was stimulated to think in terms of an electric railroad as a feeder system to the main steam railroads.

Visiting Virginia City, Yosemite and then San Francisco, he was permitted to sit on the cow-catcher of the Union Pacific locomotive— courtesy of Jay Gould—an engineer having provided him with the luxury of a cushion. He had a clear, unobstructed view, being in danger only once when the engine struck an animal thought to be a badger. Seated to one side when it struck the animal under the engine's headlight with great force, the inventor was not harmed.

By the end of August he was back in his laboratory in Menlo Park, much the better for two months of vacationing.

On January 15, 1882, James Edward Kelly made this sketch of Edison at his Goerck Street shop in New York City where John Kruesi, under Edison's direction, started what was to be the forerunner of the General Electric Company. Edison National Historic Site.

**EDISON'S GREATEST CONTRIBUTION TO TELEGRAPHY.** The quadruplex permitted sending four messages over one wire at the same time. Western Union Telegraph Company.

T. A. EDISON.
Quadruplex Telegraph Repeaters.

No. 209,241.     Patented Oct. 22, 1878.

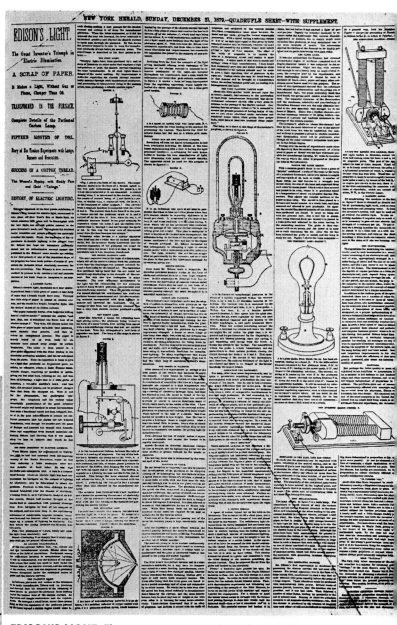

**EDISON'S LIGHT.** The newspaper scoop that released the astonishing story of Edison's successful gasless lighting. New York Public Library.

**DRESSED IN HIS BEST.** Mr. Edison cared little for clothes, never bothering to don a rubber apron or laboratory coat. His clothing soon displayed evidence of his visit to the chemistry laboratory. 1910. Library of Congress.

Chapter Seven

# Light For Everyone

In the middle of September, 1878, the New York *Sun* made public Edison's prediction that an electric light would be discovered—this in an era of gas lighting. In an interview with a *Sun* reporter late in October he visualized a central station that would deliver electricity for lighting every house in New York, and that the current would be measured and sold. In six weeks he hoped to have the new electric light ready!

Electric lighting was not a new interest for Edison. In September, 1877, he had experimented with carbon to produce practical lighting, probably influenced by his success with carbon in his development of the telephone that summer.

Arc lighting of streets and factories had been introduced at the 1876 Centennial but showed no promise for household use. Moses G. Farmer, Joseph W. Swan and W. E. Sawyer had experimented with the incandescent lamp but had failed to make it practical, the source of light disintegrating too rapidly.

On March 19, 1878, the New York *Times* announced that W. E. Sawyer had developed "a new electric light adapted to the illumination of dwellings" and that it consisted of "two carbon rods burning in a prepared atmosphere under a glass shade." This proved highly unsatisfactory.

Following the invention of the voltaic battery in the early 1800s, it was determined that heat could be produced by passing an electric current through platinum wire or pieces of carbon, and that the substance used changed from a red to a white heat.

By 1845, J. W. Starr, an American, had drawn attention to two types of incandescent lamps—one made of platinum foil under glass and in air, and another made as a carbon pencil but inclosed in a Torricellian vacuum. Many others attempted improvements but failed to produce a lamp of commercial value mainly because of the brief life of the carbon burner.

While traveling home from the West, Professor Barker interested Edison in a trip to Ansonia, Connecticut, to visit Barker's friend, William Wallace. Wallace was a manufacturer of arc lights and electric dynamos.

The two, accompanied by Professor Charles F. Chandler of Columbia University, left for Ansonia on September 8. Wallace was delighted to see them and in their honor had connected his latest dynamo to eight arc lamps. The excited Edison had a great time examining various pieces of equipment and making calculations and measurement. He arranged to take a set of Wallace's arc lamps to illuminate the Menlo Park laboratory but just before leaving he said, "Wallace, I believe I can beat you mak-

MODEL "Z" DYNAMOS—Long-waisted Mary Ann dynamos at reconstructed Menlo Park, Dearborn, Michigan. Edison National Historic Site.

EDISON'S GENERATORS AT MENLO PARK. Note the long leather belts used to turn the generators' armatures. From a Theodore R. Davis sketch in Harper's Monthly Magazine. Edison National Historic Site.

ing electric lights. I don't think you are working in the right direction."

Edison had a high regard for Wallace and, in later years, considered him one of the pioneers in electrical research for which he received little credit and from which others derived benefit.

Once back at Menlo Park Edison devoted his entire time and attention to the study of gas illumination. It was his practice to take a good look back—to read every book and article on the subject he was approaching, and then take an unprecedented and unpredictable path forward.

Making one of the first known market surveys, he made a thorough investigation of several New York City blocks to determine the number of gas lights in every building and how long each light burned. By knowing exactly what he would be competing with, he was able to decide just what manner of lighting he must provide.

The distribution system must be simple, safe, economical and adaptable to any circumstance. The lamp itself must be safe, simple, noiseless, cheaper than gas, and be able to be turned off individually, this latter characteristic not being applicable to any other form of electric illumination . His major problem would be that of subdividing the electrical current much as illuminating gas had been sub-divided by an individual pipe to each outlet.

THE FIRST INCANDESCENT LAMP FACTORY IN THE WORLD. Manufacture of lamps began in this Menlo Park building alongside the Pennsylvania Railroad tracks about one-half mile from the laboratory in October, 1880. The four men in the center foreground are, left to right: Philip S. Dyer, William J. Hammer, Francis R. Upton, James Bradley. Edison National Historic Site.

**HENRY VILLARD,** president of the Oregon Railroad & Navigation Company in 1880 and of the Northern Pacific Railroad in 1881, had Edison install a lighting plant in the **S. S. Columbia,** the first such installation in the world. It began its voyage in May, 1880, using four "Mary Ann" dynamos. Library of Congress.

At this point money was a very necessary ingredient. His friend and legal adviser, Grosvenor P. Lowrey, realized that more buildings and equipment were necessary if the discovery was to be made ahead of others. On October 24, 1878, the Wall Street firm of the Edison Electric Company was formed, with a capitalization of $300,000, half of which was immediately available to equip the laboratory.

There had been many ingenious lamps made by outstanding inventors in both Europe and America but none had been proved practical. The most practical, the arc lamp, had to be wired in series so that all lamps would have to be turned on or off at once. The light was blinding, the amperage high; they gave off unwholesome gases, and they burned in open globes.

Edison wanted to subdivide electricity so that it could be controlled to the individual lights, using the minimum of electricity. This had never been done. English scientists were loud in their denunciation of his attempts to solve the problem of the subdivision of electric current, and aired their views before an investigating committee of Parliament. General conclusions reached were "Impossible! It couldn't be done." Professor John Tyndall was the lone exception, and in a statement before the Royal

**SARAH BERNHARDT,** while touring the United States as a tragedienne, visited Menlo Park in December of 1880. She was delighted with Edison's lighting demonstration and enthralled with his tin foil phonograph, and attempted to obtain one. She thought he resembled Napoleon I physically though she considered Napoleon a destructive genius and Edison a creative genius. Library of Congress.

**JAMES GORDON BENNETT** as publisher of the New York **Herald** gave Edison considerable publicity and was one of the visiting notables at Menlo Park. 1910. Library of Congress.

**DR. NORVIN GREEN,** president of the Western Union Telegraph Company, was one of the original investors in the Edison Electric Light Company. 1878 engraving. Western Union Telegraph Company.

**FIRST INCANDESCENT LIGHTING-WIRING BILL.** November 15, 1881. Edison National Historic Site.

Institution on January 17, 1879, evidenced his faith in Edison.

Edison decided that to subdivide electrical current he must create an incandescent lamp having a high resistance with a small radiating surface, and wired so it could be turned on or off without interfering with other lamps on the line. Then it would be practical commercially.

Oxygen was recognized as the enemy of success. The oxygen in the air would burn up any substance he might use as a lamp filament. By passing a current from battery cells through a carbon filament he was able to determine how much current was needed to make it glow—to make it incandescent. The next, and biggest, problem was that of protecting it from oxygen so it would have a longer life.

The obvious answer to the problem was to shield the filament from the oxygen in the atmosphere. Placing the filament in a sealed glass globe and withdrawing all air to form a vacuum was the solution.

Edison had discovered by endless experiments that by heating platinum several times with a current it became quite hard and would emit more light. Believing this was due to gases being driven out of the platinum and causing the metal to become harder, he reasoned that still more gas could be driven out in a vacuum, thereby enabling additional light to be emitted.

Learning of an improved type of vacuum pump—the Sprengel pump—he borrowed one from Princeton College until he could obtain one from England. When Francis Upton returned with the borrowed pump he and his assistants stayed up all night trying it out. In obtaining a vacuum within one or two millimeters of full exhaustion of air, he was able to obtain a brilliant 25 candlepower light with a platinum wire filament that produced only four candlepower in open air, then melted. By further experimentation he combined the best features of the Sprengel and Geissler pumps. By October, 1879, he was able to exhaust all but one millionth of the air in a lamp bulb!

Concluding that a platinum filament would not do, he returned to carbon though he continued to use platinum lead-in wires since the metal matched glass in its reaction to heat. Carbon seemed to be the material with the greatest prospects but the problem of making it into a burner that would maintain a temperature of 2,000 degrees for 1,000 hours before

**OUR FIRST ELECTRIC RAILWAY**
went into operation May 13, 1880, at Menlo Park. Charles Batchelor is seated in front with hand on the throttle. With him on this maiden trip were: J. L. Hornig, Charles Hughes, Tom Logan, William J. Hammer, Francis Jehl, Alexander Mungle, H. V. Campbell, John W. Lawson, William Mills, John Ott, John Randolph, George Hill. Edison National Historic Site.

breaking was monumental enough. To produce it as a hair-like filament characterized by great resistance yet sturdy enough to withstand hard jarring was one thing, but to be made so it could be produced in volume at low cost for commercial use was another.

He was steadfast in his resolve to keep secret the details of his first lamp. Previously he had willingly given out details of any invention he was working on. It was while working on the telephone that description of it had reached Germany. This almost prevented him from obtaining a patent there. It was only because an essential point was not fully described that he got the patent, though the expense of obtaining it was greatly increased.

By the end of 1878, the money advanced by the Edison Electric Company was about gone and the faith of some of the backers was going too. Inviting the principal ones to Menlo Park, Edison demonstrated to them his failures, then showed them why he had failed. The lamps he used were short lived; he was convinced that he must develop one of high resistance.

One of the bankers remarked that this was the point J. W. Starr had reached years before. He believed it would have been better to have purchased a copy of the book for a few dollars and start where he left off rather than spend $50,000 to reach that point. Edison disagreed. He believed the incandescent light had been passed over by Starr, and he knew he could find it between Starr's starting and stopping point. It took Lowrey to convince the visitors they should advance another $50,000.

At this time a bewildering thing occurred. It became necessary for him to stop his research on the incandescent lamp and return to the telephone. Colonel George E. Gouraud, an Eng-

lish representative of Edison's, had organized the Edison Telephone Company in London. Bergmann had been making and sending the equipment over there and Edward H. Johnson was directing the introduction of the new carbon transmitting telephone.

Their competitors, the Bell interests, were infringing on the Edison transmitter while Edison was doing the same with the Bell receiver. The Bell interests suddenly had threatened to sue the Edison company.

Gouraud's secretary, Samuel Insull, cabled Edison of the impending suit. Edison's reply stated that "if we would wait 60 or 90 days he would supply a new form of receiver." During February and March he solved the problem; his patent application was signed March 24,

**PAGES IN AN INVENTOR'S NOTEBOOK.** On February 13, 1880, while experimenting to increase the life of his incandescent lamp, Edison made note of a carbon deposit on the sides of his lamp. Later, in 1883, he had concluded that this phenomenon—now called the "Edison effect"—involved an electrically charged carbon particle. On November 15, 1883, he applied for a patent on a lamp based on the Edison effect, which became the first electronic device patented. Edison National Historic Site.

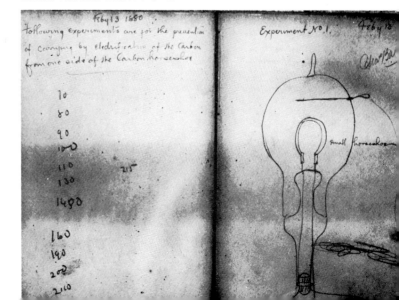

1879. What he had done was to make chalk talk.

Several years earlier (1874) he had discovered that when a block of chalk moistened with a conducting solution was connected in a circuit with a battery, a switch and a metallic brush, if the brush was drawn across the chalk block the friction decreased when the current was flowing. He applied this principle of the electromotograph to telegraph, selling it to Orton for $100,000. Now he applied this principle to the telephone receiver.

Afterward known as the loud-speaking telephone or chalk receiver, it consisted of a diaphragm and a cylinder of compressed chalk. As he described it, "A thin spring connected to the center of the diaphragm extended outwardly and rested on the chalk cylinder, and was pressed against it with pressure equal to that which would be due to weight of about six pounds. The chalk was rotated by hand. The volume of sound was very great. A person talking into the carbon transmitter in New York had his voice so amplified that he could be heard one thousand feet away in an open field at Menlo Park. This great excess of power was due to the fact that the latter came from the person turning the handle."

The Bell Company, recognizing the futility of such competition, negotiated for a consolidation, then made an offer to buy Edison's interest. Gouraud relayed their offer of "thirty thousand." Edison accepted. When the bank

**DYNAMO ROOM IN THE PEARL STREET STATION.** Sketch in **Scientific American**, August 26, 1882. Edison National Historic Site.

draft came through, he was amazed to find it was for 30,000 pounds, not dollars. He realized $150,000.

Now turning his entire energy to the incandescent lamp, Edison digressed from carbon and returned to platinum because of its strength and high fusing point. By April, 1879, he had discovered that platinum wire would emit much more light in an all-glass globe if a current was passed through the wire during the process of pumping air out of the globe. Now knowing that the wire heated by the current in it, drove the gases out of the platinum so they could be pumped out of the globe, thus decreasing its chance of melting, he reasoned that the greater the vacuum created, the higher the infusibility of the platinum filament.

He had tried out various materials for filaments such as iridium, titanium, zirconium and other rare metals, but all were too expensive for commercial use. But on April 12, 1879, he was ready to make a patent application for his first lamp using the vacuum. Except for the filament material used it basically resembled the incandescent lamp.

**A MODEL OF EDISON'S ORIGINAL CENTRAL STATION IN NEW YORK CITY.** 1882. Edison National Historic Site.

**AN UNSIGHTLY AND DANGEROUS MASS OF WIRES** darkened New York skies in 1880. Edison planned to go underground with his distribution system. Consolidated Edison Company of New York, Inc.

**LAYING UNDERGROUND TUBES FOR WIRING FROM THE PEARL STREET** central station in New York City. From a drawing in **Harper's Weekly.** 1882. Consolidated Edison Company of New York, Inc.

AN EARLY EDISON POWER STATION. He soon eliminated the leather belting and flywheel by overcoming the difficulties of combining the steam turbine with his generator. Used by permission of the General Electric Company.

It was apparent to him that in his quest for an ideal filament, the solution was not far away. On October 21, 1879, following earlier experiments with a puttylike mixture of lamp black and tar, his objective was reached.

He had been using cotton sewing thread impregnated with lamp black that had been ground with a mortar and pestle for many hours until the paste contained a powder finer than the finest flour. Once the thread was thorough-

A NEW INDUSTRY WAS BORN. All appliances for the lighting system had to be invented and manufactured such as: wooden lamp sockets (left), fuseblock (right), switchboards, dynamos, lamps, switches, meters, underground conductors and connectors, to name a few. Edison National Historic Site.

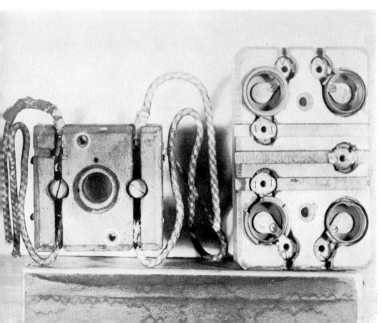

ly impregnated by kneading and rolling, it was carefully placed in a carbonizing furnace for many hours, then permitted to cool for an equal period of time. The result resembled a long black hair. The filament was attached to two platinum wires extending from a glass stem prepared by the glassblower Ludwig Boehm which he sealed into a glass bulb he had blown for that purpose.

It was Sunday morning, October 19, 1879, the day following the preparation of this particular bulb. Francis Jehl had placed the bulb on the vacuum pump he operated while Edison sat on a chair opposite him watching Jehl as he worked. When the bulb had most of its air exhausted, Edison heated the bulb with an alcohol flame, as he had done in past experiments, to expand and dry the remaining air. Then attaching the wires of the bulb to the terminals of bichromate battery cells momentarily, large bubbles of air appeared in the pump tube. This was repeated from time to time until a high degree of vacuum was evident. Gradually he had increased the intensity of the current as well as the length of time it was applied. While the pump was working and the full current was on for some time, he asked Boehm to seal off the bulb.

Its life test began about eight a.m. on October 19. Few men were around, the help being home for the day. Jehl and Charles Batchelor were the only ones with Edison at this time though Kruesi, Upton, Lawson, Force and Boehm were in from time to time to see how things were going. This was just another day and another in a long series of experiments to all of them for none suspected this would be a success.

The life test began with Edison requesting Jehl to put the newly finished lamp on the stand and begin the test. Once turned on, it continued to glow brilliantly all that night—then through the day of the 20th, the vigil continued by Batchelor, Force and Upton. That night it was Edison, Jehl and Batchelor who stood watch. Near two o'clock of October 21, 1879, the lamp continued to give forth a brilliant light. Now having succeeded, Edison gradually increased the voltage until the filament fell apart. The bulb was then taken apart and examined as had been the custom in the past.

In describing his feelings, Edison said, "We sat and watched it with anxiety growing into elation. It lasted about 45 hours, and then I said, 'If it will burn that number of hours now,

EDISON ELECTRIC RAILROAD at Menlo Park had about three miles of track constructed for testing an improved electric locomotive Edison built at the encouragement of Henry Villard. April 17, 1882. Left to right: Samuel Insull, C. Van Cleve, Charles T. Hughes. Edison National Historic

I know I can make it burn a hundred!" He "realized that the practical incandescent lamp had been born."

Not satisfied with his success at this point, he wanted something better. Everything within reach was carbonized: all kinds of papers and cardboards, twines, wood fibers, and vegetable fibers, no fewer than 6,000 species of the latter being tested. While viewing specimens under a microscope he became quite interested in bamboo fibers, an interest that sent men to Japan, China and other parts of the world in search of the ideal substance for a filament.

By early November, some of the investors in the Edison Electric Light Company learned the secret of the new lamp, though Edison had done his best to keep it under wraps. He had only applied for a patent on November 1 (It was granted January 27, 1880).

In thirteen months he had expended almost

$43,000 not counting patent expenses and was in dire need of funds. Some of J. P. Morgan's partners had seen Upton's and Edison's houses in Menlo Park lighted with the new incandescent lamps. To them it appeared to be a plaything, a toy. Edison needed money to build a power station to test out answers to many problems, yet the directors remained unimpressed. Lowrey did his best to defend Edison and, in the end, had to release the story of the secret to the public to shake the stockholders into reality.

A front-page story in the New York *Herald,* on Sunday, December 21, 1879, announced *"THE GREAT INVENTOR'S TRIUMPH IN ELECTRICAL ILLUMINATION."* Edison Electric stock rose for a time to $3,500 a share. Even then there was haggling among the stockholders, a small advance being made by them in early 1880.

THE LIGHT STILL BURNS. The greatest of his achievements was the incandescent lamp for it changed a long night into day. To progress there had to be a beginning. The ascent of the incandescent lamp is shown, left to right: Edison's first lamp, carbon filament lamp, tantalum filament lamp, drawn wire filament lamp with tip, gas-filled lamp with tip, vacuum lamp without tip, gas-filled lamp without tip, inside frosted lamp. National Youth Administration in the National Archives.

"One of the main impressions left upon me after knowing Mr. Edison for many years is the marvelous accuracy of his guesses. He will see the general nature of a result long before it can be reached by mathematical calculation," Francis Upton recalled. Falk photo, New York. 1904. Edison National Historic Site.

Chapter Eight

# Invention Factory

The midwife of fantasy had become the proud father of a reality. Edison had shaken the scientific world and amazed all others, the reaction being immediate. People poured into the hamlet by the hundreds, curious to see the "Wizard of Menlo Park" and his astonishing invention. They came from everywhere—by rail, by wagon, by carriage and on foot. The never ending stream hampered him severely for Marshall Fox, who had written the first story of the lamp—and accompanied him on his trip to Rawlins, Wyoming, the year before— had announced prematurely that Menlo Park would be electrically illuminated for New Year's Eve, 1880.

Special trains were run by the Pennsylvania Railroad, some 3,000 curious pouring into the community. Edison's entire staff of 60 had worked ceaselessly for ten days to prepare for the demonstration. The visitors saw over 400 lights illuminate the streets, four houses and the area in and around the Edison buildings.

There was a never-ending interest in turning the lights off and on. An electric motor that ran a sewing machine was a matter of great curiosity. When the inventor disconnected the wires from it and attached them to an electric lamp, the change from power to lighting created considerable comment.

Edison had used underground conductors throughout. One of the shop buildings housed the dynamo, acting as a central station. Though warned not to enter the dynamo room, several did and had their watches magnetized. In front of one of the dynamos, one of the women bent over to look at an object on the floor, and had her hairpins pulled out in doing so.

The demonstration was a great success and the public acclaim was widespread. There was a theft of eight lamps, and an attempt by a well-known electrician to drop a piece of No. 10 wire across the supply line to short-circuit it. Caught in the act by the inventor's vigilant assistants—only four lamps were darkened because Edison had devised a safety fuse to protect various lamp groupings—he was ejected to the accompaniment of appropriate language.

Edison's experiments had cost him $43,000, ending in an invention so unique and novel there were no parts available for a system necessary to operate it. Everything needed had yet to be invented—dynamos, switches, fuses, meters, insulators and insulating tape, to name a few. He had said, "Remember, nothing that's good works by itself, just to please you; you've got to make the damn thing work."

From the beginning of his lighting project he had recognized the need for a constant-amperage dynamo that would operate at 110 volts.

**THE FIRST THREE-WIRE CENTRAL STATION.** Sunbury, Pa. Operation started on July 4, 1883. Edison National Historic Site.

**THE FIRST USE OF ELECTRIC CHRISTMAS TREE BULBS** was in the home of Edward H. Johnson, New York City, as shown. Christmas, 1882. Bulbs were made at the Edison Lamp Factory, Harrison, N. J. Edison National Historic Site.

The existing dynamos of the Brush type were uneconomical and inefficient, the Brush dynamo, because of friction and air resistance, operating at 31 per cent.

Little was known about the construction of dynamos. Those already being manufactured were intended for arc lighting. Edison assigned his staff to the various problems as he visualized them and in a short time had developed a new type dynamo. Dubbed the "Long-Waisted Mary Ann," the bipolar generator at full load tested 90 per cent efficient.

Edison was bugged by belts. He recognized the loss of power from the steam engine to the dynamo through the use of drive belts. The solution was that of direct coupling. Starting with steam engines operating at 66 to 100 revolutions a minute, he graduated to a Porter-Allen steam engine with a speed of 600 revolutions. The test of this coupling ended in a ruptured steam pipe. A year later (1881) he obtained a satisfactory coupling with an engine that ran at 350 revolutions per minute, a very necessary advance if he was to successfully develop a central station with a constant source of electrical energy. Its capacity was 1,200 lamps, the previous ones being 60.

In April, 1880, Henry Villard, president of the Oregon Railway and Navigation Company as well as an investor in the Edison Electric Light Company, asked Edison to install a complete lighting plant in the newly built *S. S. Columbia*. Villard was a man well ahead of his times, his ideas being both bold and progressive.

This first commercial lighting plant was installed in the *S. S. Columbia* when she was docked at the foot of Wall Street in New York. Four "A" type "Mary Ann" generators were used, each able to supply 60 carbonized paper horseshoe filament lamps of 16 candle power each. The generators were placed in a line along the engine room wall, the power being supplied by belts and pulleys from two vertical steam engines in the next room.

Insulation on the wiring consisted of paraffined cotton, the wire being held in place on the woodwork by iron staples. After they were in place one wire was painted red for the positive pole, and the other painted blue. Fuses consisted of a lead wire in a glass tube, while the lamp sockets were of wood with two metal strips inside to which the two wires were attached.

The arc-light systems that had been installed in various cities, using the same crude installa-

**COAL DELIVERY TO THE EDISON ELECTRIC LIGHT CO. OF PHILADELPHIA.** Edison National Historic Site.

tion, had been the source of many fires. It is no wonder that marine underwriters refused to insure this ship on its maiden voyage around Cape Horn to Portland, Oregon. In spite of all the criticism and prognostications of disaster the ship made the trip without mishap, the lights and generators functioning perfectly.

The 115 paper horseshoe carbon filament lamps used were run for 415 hours until they were replaced in Portland with bamboo filament lamps. Not a lamp had burned out. The power plant continued in active service for 15 years until July, 1895, when the ship was overhauled.

As president of the Northern Pacific Railroad it was natural that Villard would ask the inventor why electricity could not be used to propel railroad engines. Edison's response was immediate and enthusiastic. He had given the subject some thought when on the trip to Wyoming in 1878. Now was as good a time as any to pursue it.

Others had worked on electric railroads before but with little progress. Dynamos and motors had not been available, and batteries had been the only source of electricity.

Edison had developed a tiny motor for use at the upper end of his electric pen, and one of his earliest demonstrations of the use of a motor in the laboratory was in the running of a sewing machine. Fox had described the motor as part of the Edison electric lighting system in his famous article of December 21, 1879, in the New York *Herald*. He wrote of it as a "Domestic Motor" capable of pumping water and running a sewing machine.

**A PAGE FROM EDISON'S DIARY.** July 12, 1885. Edison National Historic Site.

Menlo Park N.J.

Sunday July 12 1885

Awakened at 5.15 AM. My eyes were embarassed by the sunbeams—turned my back to them and tried to take another dip into oblivion—succeeded—awakened at 7 AM. thought of Mina Daisy and Mamma G— put all 3 in my mental kaledescope to obtain a new combination a la Galton. took Mina as a basis, tried to improve her beauty by discarding and adding certain features borrowed from Daisy and Mamma G, a sort of Raphaelized beauty got into it too deep mind flew away and I went to sleep again. Awakened at 8.15 AM. Poweful itching of my head, lots of white dry dandruff—what is this d——mnable material. Perhaps its the dust from the dry literary matter I've crowded into my noddle lately Its nomadic. gets all over my coat, must read about it in the Encyclopedia. Smoking too much makes me nervous—must lasso my natural tendency to acquire such habits—holding heavy cigar constantly in my mouth has deformed my upper lip, it has a sort of Havanna curl. Arose at 9 oclock came down stairs expecting twas too late for breakfast—twasn't. couldnt eat much, nerves of stomach too nicotinny. The roots of tobacco plants must go clear through to hell. Satans principal agent Dyspepsia

A lightweight track a third of a mile in length was spiked to ties laid on the ground, the rails being used to supply the power—one was used for the positive pole and the other for the negative.

The locomotive was a flatcar with a four-wheeled iron truck. On it he had mounted one of his dynamos to be used as the motor. This "long waisted Mary Ann" with its long-legged field magnet cores was the largest known, having a capacity of 60 amperes. A friction pulley was used to convey the motor power to the wheels of the locomotive. On May 13, 1880, the railroad went into operation and on June 3, the inventor filed his patent.

A number of improvements were made soon after. The friction pulley was replaced with a leather belt on a pulley to provide safer operation. The rails that first terminated at Mine Gully were lengthened an additional three miles to reach a small stream and a shack his men called Pumptown.

Newspapers made much of the electrified railroad with the result that Menlo Park became overrun with large numbers of visitors eager for a ride on the first electric railroad. Henry Villard, enamored with the idea of testing this new method of locomotion to determine if it could be adapted to areas where it was impractical to construct steam railroads, offered Edison nearly $40,000 to defray the expenses involved. Beginning this project in September, 1881, and continuing until the Northern Pacific Railroad, of which Villard was president, went into the hands of a receiver, Edison was able to make a number of improvements, satisfying himself that an electric railway was practical and economical.

He had built a passenger locomotive that would haul as many as 90 people and travel more than 40 miles an hour. The freight locomotive he had built, though slower, could pull extremely heavy loads.

Early in 1883 the Electric Railway Com-

THOMAS ALVA EDISON
AND HIS MOST IMPORTANT PIONEER ASSOCIATES
FRANCIS R. UPTON, CHARLES BATCHELOR, JOHN KRUESI & EDWARD H. JOHNSON

**EDISON AND ASSOCIATES.** November 22, 1884. Falk photo, New York. Edison National Historic Site.

**GLENMONT.** The home that Edison bought for his bride occupied a ridge overlooking West Orange, New Jersey. Edison National Historic Site.

**MINA MILLER EDISON.** Ca. 1886. The inventor and Mina Miller were married in Akron, Ohio, February 24, 1886. Edison National Historic Site.

**SECOND FLOOR LIVING ROOM AT GLENMONT.** Edison's desk is at the right; Mrs. Mina Edison's desk is on the left. Edison National Historic Site.

89

Night Ladies." Glassblower Ludwig Boehm often entertained them by playing on his zither and singing German songs.

Often there were old friends and acquaintances, or even office employees, present at these midnight gatherings, eager to enjoy the fun and frolic. Everyone enjoyed the round of stories and all were welcome to aid in the disposal of the lunch.

The long hours had their effect. Even Edison, with his known capacity for sleeplessness, would sleep on one of the laboratory tables with several books for a pillow. If one of the assistants offered objectionable snoring when the early hours of the morning found him atop one of the benches enjoying some sleep, his protesting audience would respond by using a "corpse reviver." This was a Babbitt soapbox without a cover upon which was mounted a ratchet-wheel and crank with a slab of wood resting in the teeth of the ratchet-wheel. Turning the crank produced a sound tantamount to a hurricane in a china shop.

Another penalty was the application of the "resurrector of the dead." Comparable to the "hot foot" commonly applied in the armed forces, it consisted of placing a spontaneous combustion fluid under the snorer's buttock. When the heat created by the fluid reached its peak, the sleeper would leap toward a tank of water where he could cool and soothe his hot bottom.

The laboratory boasted of two pets—one a St. Bernard dog called Wallace after the electrical pioneer William Wallace, and the other a raccoon that tried to scoop up mercury with its hands hours upon end.

At this time Edison was a pleasant looking man, five feet, ten inches tall, with piercing gray eyes, of fair complexion, his dark hair slightly silvered and usually dishevelled with the appearance of having been his own barber. He was too busy to be careful of dress. His clothes usually were the worse for wear and seemed always to be acid stained, yet when the occasion demanded it he appeared fashionable and well-dressed. Invariably his hands were discolored from some chemical. His shoes rarely were shined. He disliked honors or notoriety. His tastes were simple. Once, when taken out to dine at the fashionable Delmonico's, the meal he ordered consisted of a piece of pie and a cup of tea.

A contemporary Edison biographer, J. B.

**EDISON INDUSTRIES AT WEST ORANGE** tower over the original "invention factory." Edison Industries extend across the center of the photograph. Edison National Historic Site.

McClure, said: "In his family he is affectionate and generous, a kind husband and indulgent father, caring little for the ordinary mannerisms of life, and always reaching the point by the nearest road."

"He never put himself forward," said Francis Jehl, "as an exalted figure. In no way did he boast of being infallible. His manner created a profound respect for him from his employees and he mingled with them in an intimate manner. He possessed an irresistible personal magnetism; no one ever felt the least bit uncomfortable in his presence."

There are many evidences of his kindness and generosity. The difficulties of his youth were not so far past but what he remembered them. In 1880, a well-mannered young country boy seemed unable to carry out the instructions of one of the assistants. When the assistant asked Edison to discharge him, Edison, knowing the boy was a willing worker, sent him to John Kruesi who made a useful helper out of him.

**PHONOPLEX RAILROAD TELEGRAPH.** 1887. Edison National Historic Site.

**EDISON'S WEST ORANGE, NEW JERSEY, LABORATORY.**
This main building was built in the summer of 1887, and occupied by Edison for 44 years. Housing the library and machine shops, it is one of a group of his laboratories maintained by the National Park Service and is called the Edison National Historic Site. Edison National Historic Site.

**BOOKS AND MORE BOOKS** occupied the two floors above the library's main floor. When the inventor attacked an idea he obtained and absorbed every publication available on the subject before he began his experimentation. Edison National Historic Site.

pany of America was formed. Capitalized for $2 million to promote the patents of Edison and Stephen D. Field, it listed Edison as its consulting electrical engineer. Progress in this field was not phenomenal. By 1897, the company that had a ground floor opportunity to electrify street transportation in America voluntarily folded up.

Meanwhile, the hunt for a better material for lamp filaments continued. The laboratory was never closed. Work continued round the clock, night and day, for those were exciting times. Few failed to be inoculated by the excitement of search or discovery. The continuous presence of Edison only augmented the feeling of his loyal and industrious staff.

With all the tension and pressure, there was time for fun. The signal that Edison had planned to work through the night was the appearance of the night watchman Swanson with a midnight lunch. A generous supply of cheese and crackers, butter and ham was the bill of fare. When this welcome pause arrived, it was time for singing, yarn spinning and horse play. Once the food was disposed of, cigars were passed around, and a tune on the pipe organ was the signal for a songfest.

Some English newspaper had labeled Menlo Park an invention factory. At a time like this it appeared to be more of a social gathering. Starting with "My Poor Heart Is Sad With Its Weeping," they usually ended singing "Good

**EDISON'S LIBRARY AT WEST ORANGE** contains over 10,000 books. Though having little formal education, he knew a lot about everything. Edison National Historic Site.

**EDISON'S DESK** occupied the center of his library. It remains exactly as he left it when he passed away in October, 1931. Edison National Historic Site.

McQUEEN LOCOMOTIVE WORKS IN SCHENECTADY, N.Y., IN 1886. Edison purchased the McQueen Locomotive Works and moved the Edison Machine Works from New York to it in the latter part of 1886. This occurred while his men were out on strike. Used by permission of the General Electric Company.

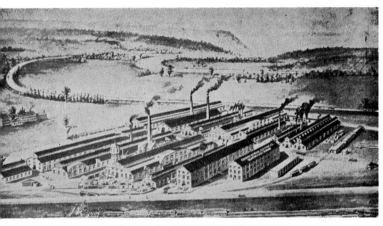

EDISON GENERAL ELECTRIC COMPANY was the result of a merger of the Edison Machine Works, the Edison Electric Light Company, the Edison Lamp Works, Bergmann & Company, Edison United Manufacturing Company, Sprague Electric Railroad and Motor Company, and the Canadian Edison Company in April, 1889. Later, in 1891, it became the General Electric Company. 1891. Used by permission of the General Electric Company.

LAMP WORKS OF THE EDISON GENERAL ELECTRIC COMPANY AT HARRISON, N. J. Its transfer to the newly formed General Electric Company came as a hard blow to Edison. Edison National Historic Site.

A year earlier, Jehl became ill with malaria. Edison noticed he was unwell and, on discovering the cause, said, "You must stop work right away, Francis, and have a change of air for a few weeks." A while later he handed him a package of quinine and a stack of currency, saying, "You must leave Menlo Park today and take the first train to Asbury Park by the ocean."

Edison loved to play doctor. He frequently drew from his vast knowledge of chemicals in providing a member of his staff with a prescription made up to fit the diagnosis he had arrived at. The success of his treatment was thought to be greater percentagewise than that of surrounding physicians.

One day a farmer came in with a problem. It seems he had 20 acres of potatoes being killed by potato bugs. Edison sent men out to obtain two quarts of bugs on which he could experiment with various chemicals. After trying a great number he discovered that carbon disulphide would kill the bugs instantly. Out at the farm he generously applied the chemical, killing all the bugs. The next morning an excited farmer informed him he had destroyed all of the potato plants. Edison settled with the farmer for $300.

Success had not lessened his interest in a practical joke. On one occasion, while experimenting with a more efficient thermopile, he picked up one Kruesi had brought in containing highly polished sulphur, gave a broad smile, then placed his left hand behind his neck and scratched his right ear, winked at Batchelor and Upton and said, "I suppose the best thing to do now is to close up the whole 'shebang,' shop and lab."

Kruesi became excited and asked why. Edison told him that the thermopile specimen was solid gold. "Gold?" exclaimed Kruesi, now bewildered. "Yes," said Edison, "Dr. Haid has tested its specific gravity and given it the acid test. It's pure gold and we can make it by the ton; our worries are over, Kruesi. We don't need the light now."

The astonished Kruesi was asked to keep it a secret which, when he agreed to, caused the group to roar with laughter. Honest John Kruesi then realized Edison had played a joke on him.

Edison hated cigarettes and prohibited their use in the laboratory, yet he could be seen each morning arriving with a cigar in his mouth. An inveterate smoker, he would have a cigar in his mouth for the entire day, smoking half of it and chewing the remainder. And in his coat pocket was a tinfoil covered package containing chewing tobacco of which he made frequent use.

It was customary for him to keep three boxes of cigars in Francis Jehl's desk, generously offering Jehl the contents for his personal use. A spittoon nearby was the object of Edison's expert aim when he was chewing tobacco.

At one time the cigars were disappearing faster than those authorized were smoking them. The inventor ordered a box of cigars made of barber shop clippings, a half-box of which were kept in Jehl's desk drawer in place of the good cigars. One evening Edison, while spitting vigorously to get something out of his mouth, remarked, "Francis, those are darn bum cigars you have in that drawer." Jehl laughingly told him the good cigars were in the photometer room just where he had ordered them placed. Edison replied, "I forgot."

Few people realize that the Edison system of lighting was planned by him down to the smallest detail. Sockets, switches, fuses, generators, distribution boxes, meters, insulators, wiring and the myriad of other items were products of his planning, foresight and genius. He knew there were no factories that could make the various items necessary to construct a successful lighting system. The Edison Electric Light Company would not go into manufacturing since it wanted to act as a holder of patents and licenses of the Edison system, so Edison was forced to go into the manufacturing business himself.

In October of 1880 he started the Edison Lamp Works in Menlo Park, the first such plant

**EDISON DYNAMO OF 1886.** A product of the Edison Machine Works in Schenectady. Used by permission of the General Electric Company.

**TALKING DOLL ASSEMBLY DEPARTMENT IN WEST ORANGE, N. J.** Edison National Historic Site.

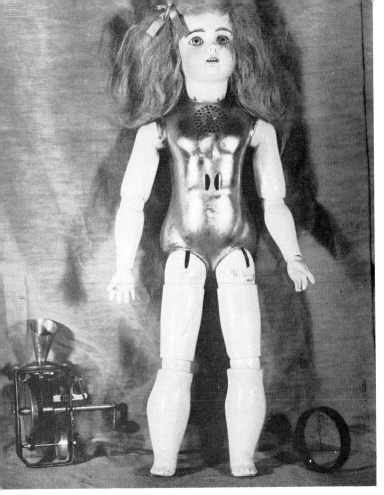

EDISON TALKING DOLL. Small phonograph to the left fitted into the back of the doll; on the right is its cylinder record. Edison National Historic Site.

THOMAS A. EDISON as he appeared June 16, 1888, after 72 hours of continuous work on this improved wax cylinder phonograph. Edison National Historic Site.

in the world, by reconditioning an old wooden building he had used to manufacture his electric pen. The lamps cost about $1.25 each to make. Then he told the Light Company if it would contract to buy them for the life of the patents, he would sell them for 40 cents each. Once the contract was completed he bought a large brick plant in Harrison, New Jersey, and moved the lamp works there in 1881.

The first year, lamps were made at $1.10 each, of which some 20 or 30 thousand sold at 40 cents each. The following year, improvements in manufacturing methods brought the cost down to 70 cents, then to 50 cents in the third year, but because of increased sales he lost a great deal of money. The cost was reduced to 37 cents the fourth year but the sales increased so much he made back all he had lost previously. When the cost got down to 22 cents, Wall Street interests bought him out.

Supplying lamps filled but one of many needs. Since financial backing was slow in appearing—Edison's bizarre and unorthodox business methods had Wall Street investors skittish—he and Batchelor sold some of their Edison Company stock to finance the Edison Machine Works. Located at 104 Goerck Street, New York, it was used for building motors and generators, principally the "Jumbos" used in Edison's first central stations. It began its operation in March, 1881.

His next move was to organize and finance the Electric Tube Company at 65 Washington Street, New York, for manufacturing underground conduit. Sigmund Bergmann organized Bergmann & Co., at 17th Street and Avenue B, New York, manufacturing fixtures, meters, junction boxes and other accessories there.

A big problem to solve was that of the lamps farthest from his generator losing as much as a third of their intensity because of the resistance of the intervening wires. Then there was the high cost of copper wire, for each lamp had separate wiring from the generator. His answer to the problem was a distribution plan calling for main wires along each side of the street and onto which the houses or street lamps were connected. The main wires would be connected at both ends, creating a loop, having equal intensity at any point. The feeder wire from the generator to it suffered the only drop in pressure, the mains being unaffected. Voltage was set at 110. Copper wire costs were reduced seven-eighths.

Edison had a dream. He wanted to install

his electrical system in New York. Bankers were resistant to the idea, wanting to see it demonstrated on a small scale, preferably at Menlo Park. There were weaknesses to correct and economy over gaslight to prove. And it was at this time he made his New York market survey. His ultimate purpose was "to devise the means of establishing electric lights on a commercial basis; to distribute the current from a central station and measure it, as gas is measured, and to bring the cost down to a point where the enormous moneyed influence of gas can be successfully encountered."

Those who supported the inventor decided it was time to illuminate the lower part of New York City. The project having been carefully studied by his staff, Edison was satisfied it would be successful. On December 17, 1880, the Edison Electric Illuminating Company of New York was organized and the signal was given him to proceed.

Blocked by indifferent politicians, criticized by a portion of the press, imitated in London by a rival, and receiving no credit in the United States for his astounding and revolutionary accomplishment, he became highly discouraged. But he was too deeply involved and too much of a fighter to quit.

Compared to today, New York and the country was in total darkness. Dim gaslights were placed at long intervals on city streets; small

AN EXHAUSTED STAFF poses with an improved phonograph just before shipment to England, June 16, 1888. Standing, left to right; W. K. L. Dickson, Charles Batchelor, A. Theodore E. Wangemann, John Ott, Charles Brown; seated, left to right: Fred Ott, Thomas A. Edison, Col. George E. Gouraud. West Orange Laboratory, N. J., 5 p.m. Edison National Historic Site.

EDISON'S ANSWER TO COMPETITION was this improved phonograph. He had informed his assistants they were to work continuously night and day with him until this model was perfect. It was — 72 hours later. June 16, 1888. Edison National Historic Site.

**EDISON PRODUCTS** covered an acre of ground at the Paris Exposition in 1889. Edison National Historic Site.

**A DISPLAY OF EDISON TELEPHONES AND PHONOGRAPHS** attracted over 30,000 people at the Paris Exposition. The new phonographs were second only to the Eiffel Tower in interest. 1889. Edison National Historic Site.

communities had none. Homes, stores and factories used kerosene lamps or tallow candles. Menlo Park was the one bright spot in the nation, its hillsides appearing like a sparkling diadem in the dark of each night.

Upton's friend, Charles L. Clarke, was placed in charge of the entire venture. Late in January, 1881, a full-scale test before electric illuminating company officials proved to them electric lights were cheaper than gas. Villard restrained Edison's enthusiastic desire to publicize their findings. Why arm their rivals? Edison had said, "Just wait a little and we'll make electric light so cheap only the wealthy can afford to burn candles!"

Edison had the central station idea in mind

at the start of his research on illumination. Renting a headquarters and showroom at 65 Fifth Avenue in New York, he installed an engine-run generator and numerous incandescent lamps. Two old buildings down at 255-57 Pearl Street were purchased for $150,000—much more than they anticipated spending—and an active campaign was begun to obtain subscribers.

New York was a city whose streets were clogged with wooden poles covered with wires for burglar alarms, stock tickers, telegraph, telephone and other services. Edison had decided to place all of his supply lines under the city streets. By the summer of 1881, while trying to lay underground tubes—to hold the

**EDISON DISPLAY AT THE PARIS INTERNATIONAL EXPOSITION IN 1889.** Edison's Magnetic Ore Separator is on the left. Edison National Historic Site.

**MUNICIPAL LIGHTING SYSTEM DISPLAY** in 1889 gave Paris Exposition visitors their first view of a central lighting station. Edison National Historic Site.

wiring—fast enough to keep up with his orders, he was summoned to the office of the Commissioner of Public Works. The commissioner advised him that five inspectors would be placed on the job with salaries of five dollars a day—to be paid by Edison.

This declaration upset and worried Edison. His men were working night and day under pressure. Now he could expect delay and harrassment by inspectors who knew nothing of electricity.

No inspectors were seen that first week. On Saturday afternoon they appeared for their pay. This was repeated each week, to Edison's complete satisfaction. To him it was worth the price not to be interfered with.

He had conceived the idea of the direct coupling of his dynamo with the steam engine supplying the power but engine builders had declared it impossible. He had done it on his locomotive so he could not see any reason why it couldn't be done. The steam engine building firm of Armington & Sims of Providence, Rhode Island, undertook the contract and, with Edison's ideas, soon solved the problem.

George Westinghouse, having produced a high speed engine of his own, had his representative ask Edison to give his engine a tryout. Edison didn't explain he was committed to Armington & Sims for a solution to his problem but instead said, "Tell Westinghouse to stick to air brakes. He knows all about them. He doesn't know anything about engines." Westinghouse responded by building dynamos. There is little doubt that the unguarded remark Edison made was the means of encouraging a huge new industry.

Realizing that larger dynamos would be a necessity, he designed one in the spring of 1881 for direct coupling with a steam engine that had a capacity of 1,200 lamps instead of 60. He had promised to display it at the Electrical Exposition in Paris.

This first one was completed and tested late that summer just four hours before the steamer left the docks for France. The 30 ton "Jumbo" generator was loaded on board just one hour before sailing time. His display of lighting in Paris caused considerable comment among scientists and electricians all over the world and resulted in a diploma of honor and five gold medals, the highest award given in the Exposition.

Meanwhile, the installation of iron tubing and its conduit in Manhattan was going slowly.

**BUFFALO BILL—WILLIAM F. CODY**—had his Wild West Show in Paris at the time of the Paris Exposition. A pork and beans breakfast and a fast ride in the Deadwood Stagecoach was his way of entertaining and thrilling the inventor. 1909. Library of Congress.

**LOUIS PASTEUR** invited Edison to the Pasteur Institute for a long talk while the inventor was in Paris in 1889. Edison had a deep respect for the French scientist. Library of Congress.

**AT THE ORE CONCENTRATING PLANT.** Edison with two unidentified men. Bechtelville, Pa. Ca. 1891. Edison National Historic Site.

Delivery of the piping was slow, necessitating the use of night crews working under incandescent lights. What had promised to be completed by mid-autumn was only one-third complete by winter; then it became necessary to close down till spring.

"The greatest adventure" of his life, as he called it, was one of the greatest gambles in history. For a square mile in lower New York City his men were placing mains and feeder wires underground to every office and residence, installing his newly invented meters, and attaching lamp bulbs to gas fixtures, all at no expense to the prospective users. There would be no charge until it all worked, and at a cost lower than gas. He was gambling his reputation and the money of his friends and backers.

By early September, 1882, he made a brief test, for he half expected some new phenomena would interfere. A careful, detailed check satisfied him.

Several days later, on a Monday afternoon in the presence of Bergmann, Clarke, Insull, Johnson, Kruesi and J. P. Morgan, he turned on the lights in the Drexel and Morgan offices. Lamps in one-third of the downtown area began to glow about 5 p.m. They appeared dim for it was daylight. As darkness fell two hours later the lamps were quite evident. New York newspapers such as the *Herald* and the *Times* were jubilant in their praise. The demand for lighting exceeded their ability to provide it since there were insufficient men trained to install the wiring.

Edison thrived on problems. One of his assistants said, "Edison seemed pleased when he used to run up against a serious difficulty.

**ROCK CRUSHERS.** In 1889, Edison displayed his magnetic ore separator at the Paris Exposition. Sixty miles west of Newark N. J. near Ogdensburg was a mountain of worked-out iron mines he began breaking up and crushing for his ore separator in 1891. Left to right: A. Muller, architect; William Kent, engineer; Thomas A. Edison; A. Ruce, engineer. Photo at Ogden Mines by Spencer Miller, October, 1891. Edison National Historic Site.

It would seem to stiffen his backbone and make him more prolific of new ideas."

One afternoon a policeman arrived at the Pearl Street station with the report there was trouble uptown. Edison personally rushed to the point of trouble where a crowd of men and boys had gathered. In his account he reported, "There was a leak in one of our main junction boxes, and on account of the cellars extending under the street, the moist top soil had become charged."

The gathering crowd, aware of the shock-giving condition of the street, watched a rag-man drive his cart and old nag around the corner as a boy called to him, "This way, old man. Watch out for the other side. Come this way." The crowd watched in silence, Edison one of them.

The ragman clucked to his horse and headed him for what he thought was a safe surface. Suddenly the horse reared high in the air, dropped down, then reared again. Its final move was like that of a race horse at the start of the Kentucky Derby. The ragman's screams and the roar of the crowd soon died down for it took but a moment for the cart to pass out of sight.

The following day a horse dealer appeared at the Pearl Street station and asked for Edison. He explained that he had seen what had happened to the ragman's horse; he wanted to buy equipment that could be used for that purpose in his stable. "We can both make a fortune out of it—buying old nags and selling them for thoroughbreds. Why, that ragman's horse was jumping around like a two-year-old."

While attending a performance of Gilbert and Sullivan's *Iolanthe* at the Bijou Theatre in Boston — the first American theatre to use electric lights—Edison noticed the lights growing dimmer. Taking Johnson with him to the power house, they discovered that Vail had allowed the fires to get low while repairing a steam leak. When Edison and Johnson failed to return to the theatre, Insull and some of the others found the two, their dress coats and plug hats on hooks, shoveling coal. Once the steam was up, they returned to the performance.

In the same year, 1882, an attorney in his employ disappeared when Edison checked with the Patent Office to see why it had not acted on his applications. He discovered they never had been filed but had been sold to others and filed under the purchasers' names—78 in all. He never gave the attorney's name, thinking it

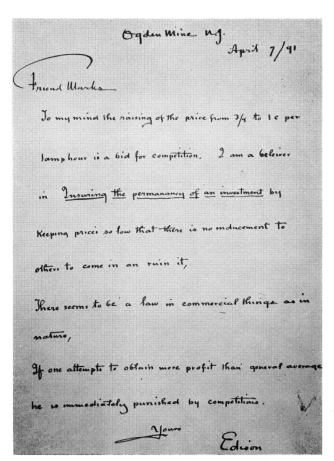

**ALWAYS A BUSINESSMAN.** April 7, 1891. Edison National Historic Site.

**THOMAS EDISON AND WILLIAM KENT AT THE OGDEN MINES.** Photo by Spencer Miller, October, 1891. Edison National Historic Site.

99

**FRONT MAN IN THE FRONT OFFICE.** Edison seated before the ore-milling office of the New Jersey and Pennsylvania Concentrating Works, Edison, New Jersey. Kreidler photo, 1895. Edison National Historic Site.

**AFTER A STORY** at the ore concentrating plant. Left to right: Walter S. Mallory; reporter Theodore Waters (McClure's Magazine); Thomas A. Edison. 1897. Edison National Historic Site.

might hurt his family.

He had some new ideas about wiring in the latter part of 1882. Following successful tests he was granted patents March 20, 1883, on a three-wire system that saved about two-thirds in copper. The first place selected to test the three-wire system was Brockton, Massachusetts, the home of Mrs. Villard's father.

The unceasing search for a better filament continued, finally settling on carbonized bamboo, a material used in all of his lamps for nearly ten years.

In early 1880, Edison had noticed that light bulbs blackened on the inside of the glass. Following a series of observations he concluded that the black deposit was due to electrically charged particles of carbon thrown from the negative side toward the positive side as tiny particles, frequently showing the white outline of the filament. Though no one understood why, Edison attributed it to a molecular bombardment caused by residual gas in contact with the hot filament. It became known as the "Edison Effect." In his patent application of November 15, 1883, he writes: "This current I have found to be proportioned to the degree of incandescence of the conductor or candlepower of the lamp." This patent, No. 307,031, is the first in the modern art of electronics.

In 1897, the British physicist Sir J. J. Thomson proved that the Edison Effect was the result of negative electrons being discharged from the hot filament. Thus Edison became the "Father of Electronics," for, in rapid succession, by applying the Edison Effect, the English physicist Sir John Fleming and the engineer Lee DeForest developed a vacuum tube that would generate radio waves. This tube, or audion, was patented by DeForest in 1907.

Edison, by publishing his observations, made the principle available, thus opening the door for the research and development of vacuum tubes including the Xray.

Mary Stilwell Edison had been a good wife. A gentle, simple soul of limited education, she had adapted herself to her husband's unusual habits. In the latter part of their married years they grew apart, he becoming more involved in his manifold interests and she in those of her household and her close friends.

Their first child, a girl, was born in 1873. Though christened Marian, her father called her "Dot." Thomas Jr., born in 1876, was promptly dubbed "Dash." Their third child, born in 1878, was named William Leslie.

ORE CONVEYOR AT ORE CONCENTRATING WORKS near Ogden, N. J. Ca. 1895. Edison National Historic Site.

ORE CONCENTRATING WORKS POWERHOUSE. Ca. 1895. Edison National Historic Site.

Mary Edison, following several years of illness, spent a few weeks with her husband at the Magnolia Hotel in St. Augustine, Florida, in April, 1884. In July she contracted typhoid fever. Suddenly growing worse after appearing to improve, she passed away on the morning of August 9, 1884.

The months that followed found him buried in his work. He spent a great deal of time with his three children or in enjoying his books or in picking out tunes on his piano he had heard at the opera or the theatre.

While in Boston installing special lamps in the Bijou Theatre, he met an old telegrapher friend, Ezra T. Gilliland. One evening at his home he was introduced to beautiful Mina Miller, the daughter of Lewis Miller, a successful Ohio inventor. Well-educated, accomplished

NEW JERSEY AND PENNSYLVANIA CONCENTRATING WORKS EMPLOYEES. W. K. L. Dickson photo. Ca. 1895. Edison National Historic Site.

**OUR BOYHOOD AMBITIONS.** H. T. Webster cartoon, 1915. Edison National Historic Site.

**EDISON AND FRIEND AT THE OGDEN MINES.** Ca. 1895. Edison National Historic Site.

**TESTING EDISON STORAGE BATTERIES.** George Meister takes Mr. Edison for a ride in the second model of a Studebaker Electric powered by Edison storage batteries. 1909. Edison National Historic Site.

and traveled, the "handsome brunette of twenty" soon overcame the 18-year difference in their ages.

The following summer, the thought of her gave him no rest. On February 24, 1886, they were married in the front parlor of the bride's Akron, Ohio, home by Dr. E. K. Young of the Methodist Episcopal Church. A blissful two-month honeymoon at Fort Myers, Florida, was spent in ignoring the many letters and telegrams from his associates urging him to return to his laboratory.

Edison had no further use for Menlo Park. He had purchased a new chateau at West Orange, New Jersey, in Llewellyn Park. On their return from Fort Myers they stopped in Akron for several weeks, then went on to this new home they called Glenmont.

While gazing from its windows he drew attention to the view of the beautiful valley below, telling his private secretary A. O. Tate he intended dotting it with factories. Edison always had dreams of being an industrialist.

THOMAS A. EDISON,
Central Station, Construction Dep't.,
No. 65 FIFTH AVENUE,

New York, Nov 1 1883

Friend Chandler

Do you know the address of a 1st Class foreman of construction who is used to city work. Perhaps WU have some, want a pusher who has brains, who wears an 8 3/8 hat & reads Plato in the original greek.

Yours

Thos A Edison.

**HANDWRITING OF THOMAS A. EDISON IN 1883.** Edison National Historic Site.

**THE S. S. COLUMBIA** carried the first commercial installation of incandescent lighting. The 3,200 ton 334 foot long vessel had four bipolar "Mary Ann" dynamos and 115 carbon paper filament lamps installed while docked at the foot of Wall Street. Departing in May, 1880, for its two months voyage around Cape Horn to San Francisco, not one of its lamps gave out in the 415 hours of continuus service. Courtesy of Gordon Newell.

Chapter Nine

# Something For Everyone

Edison was having labor trouble. Where he had dozens of workers he now had hundreds. By 1888 he would employ almost 3,000. When his shops were small his men were expected to work 18 hours a day but were paid a bonus for additional effort. Since they liked him and found the work interesting and even exciting, they did not complain.

When the lamp manufacturing started it became necessary to train additional men several months in the art of sealing in the filament. When these employees numbered 80, they formed a union and made evident their independence.

Secretly, Edison developed and manufactured 30 machines that would do the operation. When the labor agitator was fired, the union promptly went on a strike. While they were out, Edison installed his new filament sealing machines. The union never was invited back. An additional benefit was the lowering of the manufacturing costs of his lamps.

The inventor had raised the pay of his workmen at the Edison Machine Works in New York 25 cents a day. There were some who thought they could obtain more by striking. While the men were out, Edison purchased two brick buildings in Schenectady from the McQueen Locomotive Works, moving all his machinery

there. Later his men said they would like to come back to work, so he told them they could. When they showed up at the Goerck Street shops they found them empty.

It seemed to be an open season for infringers and competitors, the competitors usually being the infringers. Everyone wanted to get into the act and many were individuals who had been Edison's guests at Menlo Park and had been shown all of the advancements unselfishly. A series of suits instituted by the Edison Electric Light Company legal staff—the chief defendant being George Westinghouse—continued for many years.

Edison had little faith in patent litigation for he had concluded there was no justice in patent laws and that a patent was "simply an invitation to a lawsuit." Two million dollars in legal fees later, with two years of patent life remaining, Edison won a clearcut decision establishing him as having made the "grand discovery in the art of electric lighting." No wonder he had lost all faith in patents.

With the purchase of property in Schenectady, Henry Villard introduced the idea of a consolidation with some of their competition so they might terminate much of their "fierce competition and low prices." Edison thought prices already too high and that they could be

**OPPOSITE**—He selected assistants above average intelligence for he wanted people around him who grasped his ideas quickly. They had to be men he could trust and delegate work to. He had no use for the stupid, careless or lazy. Charles James Fox photo, Orange, New Jersey. 1927. Library of Congress.

THE WORLD'S FIRST MOTION PICTURE CAMERA, as illustrated, was completed by Edison in 1889 and called a Strip Kinetograph. It used horizontal film strips. Edison National Historic Site.

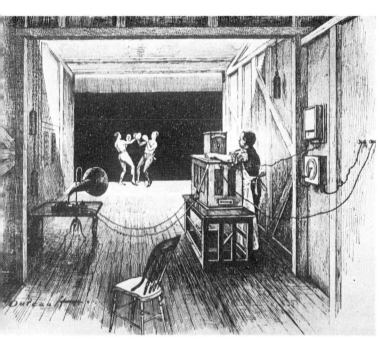

BLACK MARIA'S STUDIO STAGE. Note Edison's early attempt to tie in sound on his movie set. Drawing by R. F. Outcault in The Electrical World, June 16, 1894. Edison National Historic Site.

THE FIRST MOTION PICTURE STUDIO IN THE WORLD. Built by Edison in 1893 on the West Orange Laboratory grounds, it promptly was dubbed the "Black Maria." Edison National Historic Site.

lowered if the "leaden collar of the Edison Electric Light Co. around me" would be broken.

Under the management of Insull and Kruesi the Schenectady plant was rapidly expanding its sales and buildings. Merger seemed to be the solution to sharp competition. Previously, in 1889, Villard had engineered consolidation of all the Edison interests into what had been named the Edison General Electric Company, Edison owning about 10 per cent of its stock. The newly proposed merger involved the Thomson-Huston Co., the Edison G. E.'s principal competitor.

Unknown to Edison, the consolidation engineered by J. P. Morgan was confirmed on April 15, 1892, the new company to be called the General Electric Company. The Morgan skullduggery left Villard, Insull and Edison out in the cold.

Meanwhile, Edison had begun construction at West Orange, New Jersey, of his largest and best equipped laboratory. It was his plan to have everything he needed in the way of equipment, materials and qualified technical assistants at "a place in which you could invent anything that came into your head regardless of expense." With a staff varying from 45 to 60 assistants he could delegate many of the tasks, permitting him to carry on a variety of experiments in an executive capacity. Now 40 years of age, passionately pursuing a multitude of ideas, he had highly developed his remarkable facility for switching from one subject to another, relentlessly following any new finding his assistants might turn up in their daily progress reports. As he had said, "In trying to perfect a thing, I sometimes run straight up against a granite wall a hundred feet high. If, after trying and trying, I can't get over it, I turn to something else. Then, someday . . . something happens in some part of the world, which I recognize may help me to scale at least part of that wall."

Chichester Bell and Charles S. Tainter, on May 4, 1886, had received a patent on a process of recording on wax or a similar substance. The final result was a wax-covered paper cylinder that was played back on an instrument they introduced in the spring of 1887 as the "Graphaphone." The inventors came to Edison with a proposition that they combine their ideas, they financing further experimentation and exploitation, for which they would derive a half interest in the enterprise. Edison angrily

**CORBETT AND COURTNEY FIGHT IN THE BLACK MARIA.**
One of the first film strips was made of this staged match;
the camera was able to hold less than a minute and a half
of film. Ca. 1894. Edison National Historic Site.

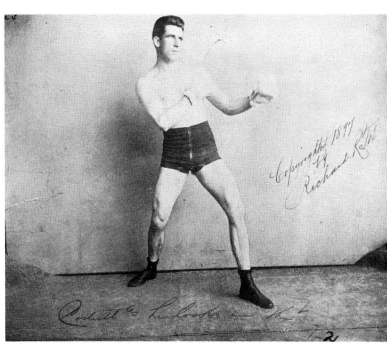

**JAMES J. CORBETT** was the boxing sensation of the 1890s.
Gentleman Jim, as he was known, was one of the first celebrities filmed by Edison. 1897. Library of Congress.

**INTERIOR OF THE PEEPHOLE KINETOSCOPE** showing the
spool bank. 1894. Edison National Historic Site.

**EDISON'S PEEPHOLE KINETOSCOPE WITH SOUND AT-
TACHMENT** used a positive print from a negative roll of
film. The action was viewed through a peephole as shown.
1894. Edison National Historic Site.

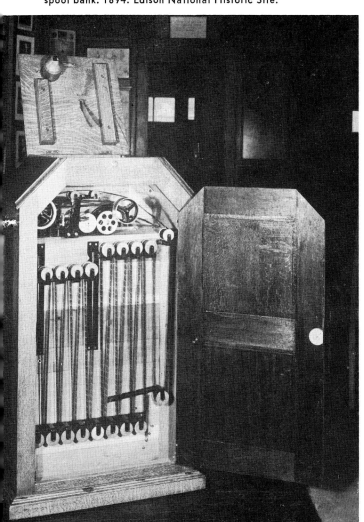

**THE PEEPHOLE KINETOSCOPE WAS ENJOYED BY MAN OR MONKEY.** All early Edison movies were made on 35 mm. film. Edison National Historic Site.

**KINETOSCOPE, PHONOGRAPH AND GRAPHOPHONE ARCADE** at 946 Market Street, San Francisco; a Peter Bacigalupi Amusement Center about 1895. The coin-operated peep show usually cost five cents and lasted one minute and 20 seconds. Edison National Historic Site.

turned them down for he believed they had pirated his invention.

Having concluded his legal agreements with the Edison Electric Light Company, the shock of the Bell-Tainter offer stirred him to spending a great part of 1887 on improving his first love, the phonograph. Near the end of the year he incorporated the Edison Phonograph Toy Company for $600,000. Dolls made in Europe were shipped to West Orange to have their vocal equipment installed. Sales for these high-priced dolls zoomed all over the world

By constant experimentation he developed a wax composition cylinder on which the recording was engraved with a cutting tool instead of the old needle, a blunt sapphire stylus being used for reproduction. The cylinder wall was one-fourth inch thick, the groove in the wax being cut to a depth of one thousandth of an inch.

His occupation with changes in the phonograph was interrupted momentarily on May 31, 1888, by the birth of a daughter, Madeline, the first of three children by his second wife.

Interested in everything new, Edison had ordered, on May 30th, 1888, a $25 Kodak camera from the Eastman Dry Plate Company of Rochester. On September 2, W. K. L. Dickson, his chief assistant, ordered a roll of Kodak film and inquired about films of higher sensitivity for Edison had an idea he wished to explore.

The "Wheel of Life" was a very popular toy at that time. It consisted of a cardboard wheel with a series of drawings along the outer edge which, if spun and looked at through a slit, would appear to move. In playing with it one day, Edison got an idea. In reading everything on the subject he could obtain, he discovered that Leland Stanford, in 1878, had a series of cameras set up along a race track to take sequence pictures to determine if all four hoofs of a running horse were on the ground at any one time.

Deciding that a large number of small pictures could be reproduced rapidly, Edison began searching for a camera capable of taking 20 to 40 pictures a second. He had considerable difficulty in obtaining sharp, clear-cut pictures but made some progress by placing those he had on the outer edge of a rotating wheel and viewing a given point while the disk rotated. The darkroom over the laboratory was off limits to everyone other than two assistants selected to carry on experiments under his instructions when he was not there.

He had improved upon his carbonized bamboo filament that year by developing and patenting a cellulose that could be squirted through a die, producing a more durable and economical filament. He had improved his phonograph and wax cylinders, organizing two companies to produce and sell them commercially. And now the spring of 1889 found him a bit tired and in need of a change of scenery. What better place, said his young and pretty wife, than a trip to Europe.

Sailing on the French liner *LaBourgogne* on August 3, 1889, he was feted and honored wherever they went. Though courteous to all he refused to make any speeches. His wife enjoyed it, while he was wearied by all of it. His major interest was the Paris Exposition; his delight was the opportunity of meeting many scientists and inventors.

Arriving in New York on October 6th, thoroughly rested and relaxed, he hurried to West Orange for he wanted to know what Batchelor and Dickson had accomplished behind the locked doors of his darkroom. Dickson seated him in a darkened room opposite a projection screen while he proceeded to turn the crank of an optical projector that cast a flickering image of Dickson on the screen as it said, "Good morning, Mr. Edison; glad to see you back. I hope you are satisfied with the *Kinetophonograph*." The greeting came from a phonograph attached to the projector—the first talking picture!

While at the Paris Exposition Edison had sent a crew of young men on an expedition to survey a 25-mile strip of land reaching from Canada to North Carolina. Equipped with extremely sensitive magnetic needles he had devised, they were to keep records of 1,000 foot intervals and indicate any reactions to magnetic bodies of ore.

He was amazed to learn of the large quantities of ore they discovered. From this survey he selected 3,000 acres in Sussex County in northwest New Jersey, which he estimated contained 200 million tons of ore. To this he added 16,000 acres containing enough iron ore to supply the United States and its export trade for 70 years.

Eastern ironmills had a crying need for low-priced high-grade ore. With this fabulous supply practically next door to the mills, he divided his problem of supply into three parts. He would have to tear down the ore-containing mountain, grind it into powder, and separate

**EDISON'S PROJECTION KINETOSCOPE OF 1896** was a step forward since it permitted large audiences to watch together. It meant the end of the peephole parlor period. Edison National Historic Site.

**AN EXPERIMENTAL EDISON MOTION PICTURE WiTH SOUND.** W. K. L. Dickson plays the violin while staff members dance. Edison National Historic Site.

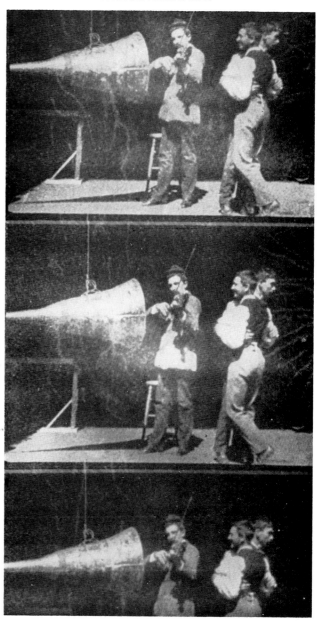

# ...THE 1898 MODEL...
# Edison Stereo=Projecting Kinetoscope.

### Send for Descriptive Catalogue.

The Edison Projecting Kinetoscope with Stereopticon attachment, illustrated above, is complete with 2 objective lenses and 2 condensers, 1 lamp serving for both lenses. Electric, calcium or acetylene light can be used with good results.

Price of machine as per illustration and with Resistance Coil — **$100.00**

Stereopticon Attachment alone and Instructions for converting Projecting Kinetoscope into a combined machine — **$25.00**

### ...ANY ONE CAN MAKE THE CHANGE...

This machine is similar to the Edison Projecting Kinetoscope with the addition of the Stereopticon attachment, which can be used for illustrated songs and regular stereopticon views. The titles and a brief description of the films can be thrown on the screen, while the films are exhibiting, or to keep the attention of the audience while changing films.

**SOMETHING DIFFERENT WAS ADDED.** Reading this catalogue page reveals the addition of a stereoptican slide attachment that has many novel uses. Edison National Historic Site.

**EDISON IN HIS WEST ORANGE LIBRARY WITH AN IMPROVED MOVIE PROJECTOR.** 1905. Edison National Historic Site.

the iron from the rock, accomplishing this at a cost low enough to make the operation commercially feasible.

Setting up an office at his mine near Ogdenburg, New Jersey, in 1890, he constructed 50 cottages, then advertised their attractiveness and low rent. The ad in the New York newspapers brought over 650 responses. So began the town of "Edison."

The usual procedure was to blast the ore-bearing rock into small boulders before it was crushed. Believing dynamite to be too expensive, he devised great rollers — called Giant Rolls — to crush rocks the size of a piano and often weighing as much as eight tons. A pair of these 70-ton rollers, each being five feet long and six feet in diameter and covered with steel knobs, were set 15 inches apart on a huge frame. The rollers were run in opposite directions by a steam engine at a speed of 60 miles an hour as huge rocks were guided through a hopper into them and ground to the size of grapefruit. At the moment the huge rock contacted the Giant Rolls the drive belts were disengaged by a slipping friction clutch mechanism he had invented. This ingenious device permitted the momentum of the heavy rollers to complete their crushing operations without damaging the steam engine.

Conveyors carried the rocks to a series of intermediate rollers and then to another of his inventions, the Three High Rolls, which crushed the rock into fine powder. This was carried to a tower to be dropped past 480 huge magnetic separators which drew the iron particles to one side and permitted the sand to go on. The concentrated ore then passed on to the mixing house where it was combined with a resinous binder, pressed into briquettes, baked and then shipped off in railway cars.

The first trial of the new briquettes occurred in 1892 for Edison had to devise and invent all of his machinery up to that point, excepting steam shovels, dynamos and engines. The briquettes did not test well so he conducted several thousand experiments to perfect them. The plant shut down for three or four years during the great depression starting in 1893, but by 1897 he began receiving orders from iron and steel mills. Then the bottom dropped out!

He had been losing thousands of dollars a day on his ore shipments in his attempt to get costs down to meet competition. In the winter of 1899 he was preparing for heavy production when he was shown a newspaper article announcing large-scale open-face iron ore mining in the Mesabi Range along the Minnesota shore of Lake Superior. When Andrew Carnegie and his associates brought the price of pig iron below ten dollars a ton, Edison knew he was through competing. He had spent a million and a half dollars, obtained mostly from the sale of his GE stock, and was in debt $300,000. This debt he intended paying off to the last cent, saying, "No company I was ever connected with has ever failed to pay off its creditors."

He was now 53 and had plans of using all of his equipment and technical knowledge to design and operate a modern portland cement works. And when he thought of the money he had spent gaining that technical knowledge, he said, "Well, it's all gone, but we had a hell of a good time spending it!"

Edison reasoned that cement would be the most useful construction material of the future. He believed "wood will rot, stone will chip and crumble, bricks disintegrate, but a cement and iron structure should last forever."

Simultaneously conducting a thorough study of cement manufacturing and storage battery construction, he soon reached a point where he knew he could make a better cement than that being manufactured. By adding some new ideas to the vast experience he had gained grinding a mountain into dust, he decided to break into the cement making industry.

Walter S. Mallory was the man selected to

**A STILL FRAME FROM "THE GREAT TRAIN ROBBERY."** The first popular film story produced by Edison (1903) for projection on the screen, it did much to stimulate the spread of nickelodeons across the country. Edison National Historic Site.

**HOLDUPS WERE COMMON** in the first series of films produced by Edison. This is a still from "The Great Train Robbery." 1903. Edison National Historic Site.

**BRONX MOVIE STUDIO OF THOMAS A. EDISON, INC.** This large glass studio, built for $100,000, was one of the first in a new industry. Edison delegated its management to others for he disliked the low artistic standards set by film producers and distributors. 1908. Edison National Historic Site.

**THE HOME MOVIE PROJECTOR (KINETOSCOPE)** was the beginning of a new hobby. Mr. Edison examines his invention. July 19, 1912. Edison National Historic Site.

manage the new industry for he had proven his managerial ability at the ore-separating plant. Following the purchase of a tract of limestone rock in eastern Pennsylvania in 1899 and the incorporation of the Edison Portland Cement Company, Edison went to his drafting board. For two days and a night he laid out his plans for the proposed plant. It had provisions for crushing, grinding, screening, sizing, weighing, mixing, drying, packaging and storing.

Disregarding the old-style kilns that were 60 feet long and 6 feet in diameter and turned out 200 barrels of cement a day, he devised a kiln 150 feet long and 9 feet in diameter that revolved on roller bearings. The cement plant with its rollers, conveyors and kilns was to be over half a mile in length and would be geared to produce a thousand barrels of cement every 24 hours.

When the plant was nearly ready to begin operation, Edison arrived to inspect it. For seven hours he went over it from crusher to packing house, making no notes. On arriving home he stayed up all that night until the following afternoon, writing his suggestions. Some 6,000 were listed and numbered so they could be carried out and reported on by number as they were acted upon. Such was his remarkable memory.

There were many problems that first year for the first production was only 400 barrels a day. His competitors had predicted failure but soon modeled after him when his production reached 1,100 barrels daily.

Several innovations were added — what today would be called quality control. Cement-rock and limestone had to be accurately proportioned in the manufacture of fine cement.

**SCENE FROM "THE PIT" AT THE BRONX STUDIOS.** H. Cronjager photo, September 10, 1912. Edison National Historic Site.

**SCENE IN BRONX MOVIE STUDIO.** 1913. National Archives.

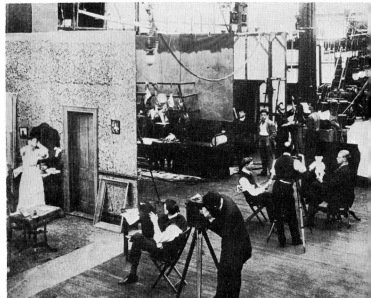

**GEORGE EASTMAN AND THOMAS A. EDISON** examine a professional motion picture camera. 1928. George Eastman House Collection.

**EDISON HOME MOVIE ADVERTISEMENT** showing the first home projector to use safety film. 1912. Edison National Historic Site.

**THE FIRST JUKE BOX.** Printed card on the case reads, "Drop a nickel in the slot—Turn crack gently till it stops." Then you got your nickel's worth. Edison National Historic Site.

**EDISON'S SUPER KINETOSCOPE.** This 1915 projector was the answer to the theatre owners' desire for quality projection. 1915. Edison National Historic Site.

Measurement usually was done by wheelbarrow loads. Edison had his scale weights set and the materials fed by a hopper that automatically stopped when the scale beam tipped an electrical connection. And he raised the quality of cement by grinding it so fine it would pass through a 200-mesh screen—10 per cent finer than the standard. It was just a matter of time before his plant became the fifth largest producer of cement in the country.

Then came his idea of pouring an entire house of concrete. Here too he was told it could not be done—a statement he went about as usual to disprove.

By 1906 he had built 12 concrete and steel buildings around his West Orange laboratory. He had developed a free-flowing concrete mix by 1908. Why not use it in a cast-iron mold of a six-room house that could be poured in six hours and be ready for occupancy in three days? Expending $100,000, he proved to his satisfaction it could be done complete with stairways, inner walls, laundry and bath tubs, wiring and piping. Then he dropped the idea after obtaining a patent on it.

In November, 1895, Professor W. K. Roentgen announced his discovery of the X-ray. Edison along with many other investigators gave it their immediate attention. In an examination of 8,000 different chemicals he found several hundred that would fluoresce. Soon he discovered that calcium tungstate, if fused to the inside of a glass vacuum tube containing an X-ray electrode, would fluoresce when exposed to the X-rays. The June, 1896, issue of the *Electrical Engineer* mentions his fluorescent lamp, the April issue showing his fluoroscope in use. One of his fluoroscopes he sent to Professor Michael Pupin of Columbia University who used it to demonstrate shotgun pellets in a man's hand. This same Edison fluoroscope was used by a surgeon to successfully perform the first fluoroscopic surgery in America.

Nothing was known of secondary radiation or the accumulative effects of X-rays at that time. Edison's assistant glassblower, Clarence Madison Dally, began to display evidence of radiation damage in the form of alopecia (loss of hair) and then ulcerations and gangrene. Following a number of amputations, he died.

Even Edison suffered ill-effects—the doctors attributed his severe eye trouble (from which he completely recovered) to overexposure to X-rays. Edison decided to drop the project of fluorescent lighting.

Though Edison had filed a caveat in October, 1888, describing "an instrument which does for the eye what the phonograph does for the ear" he had labeled a Kinetograph, it was a year later, on his return from the Paris Exposition, that Dickson was able to demonstrate an improvement on the original concept for which Edison had given explicit instructions before he had left the country.

During the early summer of 1889 Edison designed a camera through which a narrow strip of film would move across the lens through rollers. The film had perforations on one side that engaged in a sprocket wheel turned by hand, and later by a clock spring mechanism. The film moved intermittently for proper timing of the exposure, taking 46 photographs a second. The first film was three-fourths inch wide but it was increased to one and three-eighths inches—the standard 35 mm film of today—permitting perforations to be placed along each edge. This held the film steadier for the short exposures. Inventing a rotating shutter geared to admit light for a brief exposure, then permitting the film to jerk forward for the next exposure while the shutter closed off the light, permitted a series of

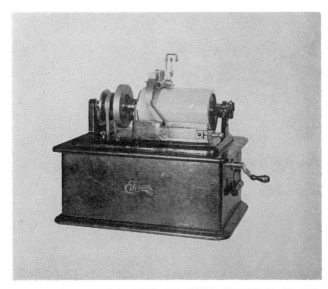

KINETOSCOPE RECORDING MACHINE INVENTED BY EDISON FOR USE WITH MOVIE FILM. This was introduced for talking motion pictures. 1913. Edison National Historic Site.

EASTMAN HOUSE PARTY IN ROCHESTER, N. Y. Left to right, seated: Mrs. Ogden Reid, George Eastman, Thomas A. Edison, Mrs. Thomas A. Edison, General John Pershing; standing: Adolph Ochs, Mrs. Charles Edison, Charles Edison, Dr. Henry F. Osborn, General James G. Harbord, Mrs. John E. Sloane, Owen D. Young, John E. Sloane, Ogden Reid. 1928. Edison National Historic Site.

photographs that gave the illusion of motion.

Already he had developed a Kinetoscope, or peep-show, consisting of a large cabinet in which revolved a motor-driven drum on which a strip film of positive prints could be viewed through a small lens. As the battery-driven motor moved the series of pictures in front of the eye, persistence of vision gave the illusion of motion. The Kinetoscope created quite a sensation across the country wherever it was shown commercially.

The appeal of moving pictures to Edison was their educational possibilities rather than their money making potential. From the beginning he had the thought of combining the motion picture camera with the phonograph. The synchronization of the two created a variety of problems which, Dickson wrote, "would have broken the spirit of inventors less inured to hardship and discouragement than Edison."

Edison believed that the synchronized recording to the lives and voices of great men and women in the world would have an impact on the study of history and economics. His interest centered in the educational field rather than on entertainment but educators failed to respond to his advanced ideas on visual education.

It was not until July, 1891, that he applied for patents on his Kinetoscope and Kineto-

**THE EDISON PHONOGRAPH USED FOR DICTATION.** Using a set of earphones attached to the machine, the inventor listens to a letter recorded on a wax cylinder. He fervently hoped the phonograph would be used in the business world first, little dreaming the impact it would make in the entertainment world. W. K. L. Dickson photo, 1893. Edison National Historic Site.

graph, or camera. His mind had been occupied with a variety of problems in the phonograph business, and in the fields of ore separation and the manufacturing of electrical equipment. Yet he continued to keep a team of four men working secretly on ideas of his that improved upon the peep show.

In 1893, Thomas Lombard, the promoter of Edison coin operated phonographs, urged him to construct a coin operated Kinetoscope. Edison responded by manufacturing 25 of them to operate at a nickel a view.

The camera for making the motion pictures was labeled the Kinetograph. The first subjects were Fred Ott sneezing, an Italian organ grinder and his monkey, Carmencita dancing and a man smoking a cigar. These were made with the illumination of four parabolic manganese lamps.

On February 1, 1893, he finished constructing a wooden building in the yard of the West Orange laboratory. Having decided to use sunlight for illumination in his movie making, he designed the building so it swung on pivots like an old-fashioned river bridge. The stage inside could follow the sun which was permitted to enter through a special opening in the roof. This Kinetographic Theatre—the first motion picture studio in the world—was an oblong building, 50 feet long. Covered with black tar paper and painted black inside to inhibit reflections, it was quickly dubbed "Black Maria" by the staff.

A variety of subjects was used in the movie shorts, the average showing time being one minute and 20 seconds. Featured were Japanese dancers, Sandow the strong man, Buffalo Bill and his Wild West show, acrobats, knife throwing acts, cockfights and occasional celebrities like Gentleman Jim Corbett. Celebrities were paid 50 dollars; ordinary performers 10 dollars. Some documentaries — the earliest known — were made.

In early 1894, Lombard along with Norman C. Raff and Frank Gammon organized the Kinetoscope Company and contracted with Edison for a large number of his peep-shows at $200 each to be exhibited in Kinetoscopic Parlors. The contract price included the film and coin operation boxes.

It soon became apparent that it was difficult to have large numbers of viewers move from box to box to see a one minute show. The answer was a projection of the motion picture on a sheet; in that manner large numbers could view it together.

**AUTOMATIC JUKE BOX ASSEMBLY DEPARTMENT.** West Orange Laboratory, 1890. This was the beginning of a coin-operated juke box industry. Ander photo. Edison National Historic Site.

**EDISON HAS A BIRTHDAY.** February 11, 1912. Edison National Historic Site.

At first Edison would have no part of the idea. Then in 1896 Thomas Armat developed a projection lantern called the Vitascope. Longer films were being used and placed on reels for ease of handling. Edison's promised screen machine had not matured so Raff made a deal with Armat so it would not "fall into the hands of parties unfriendly to you and us," he advised Edison. By adroit handling of Edison and Armat, Raff convinced them that the Edison company should manufacture the movie projector under Edison's name "in order to secure the largest profit in the shortest time." Both agreed.

In anticipation, many theaters were opened for the new Vitascope projector and wall screen. The first showings were a sensation. By 1909 there were 8,000 nickelodeons in the country—another major industry.

The first story produced in the Black Maria came out in 1903 as *The Life of an American Fireman*. The screen classic that immediately followed and was released in 1904 was *The Great Train Robbery*. This alone is worth the trip to the Edison National Historic Site at West Orange, New Jersey, for the film is shown each day.

Competition was keen but the Edison film company soon acquired a $100,000 studio in the Bronx—about 1905—under the name of Thomas A. Edison, Inc. A second New York studio—1910—was added but Edison lost interest in the commercial aspects of the growing enterprise, delegating his interest to others.

On the morning of February 17, 1913, he demonstrated his new Kinetophone in a New York theatre by projecting a scene from Shakespeare's *Julius Caesar* synochronized with an Amberola phonograph that reproduced the actors' voices for seven minutes of the one hour silent movie. The operator in the projection booth regulated the speed of the phonograph behind the screen with a long fish line when the sound got out of register with the gestures or facial expressions of the actors.

A short time prior to this Edison wrote to George Eastman to determine if he was interested in a nonflammable film for his newly invented home movie projector, and if he would like to sell the Edison projector through Eastman dealers. Eastman answered "yes" to both questions.

As usual, Edison ideas were being infringed on and litigation was pending. His competitors were many, but Judge Christian Kohlsaat of the U.S. Court in Chicago, on October 24, 1907, ruled that cameras used by William M. Selig infringed on the Edison patent. Following that

**A DISTINCTIVE HANDWRITING.** Edison wrote each letter separately, a style he developed so he could take down telegraphic press reports quickly, clearly and effortless. A letter to John Fritz, South Bethlehem, Pa. Edison National Historic Site.

**AND THEN THERE WERE TIMES** he wrote like the rest of us. "The almighty knew his business when he apportioned milk. He is the best chemist we have. Edison." Edison National Historic Site.

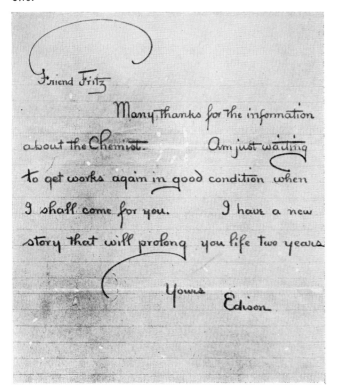

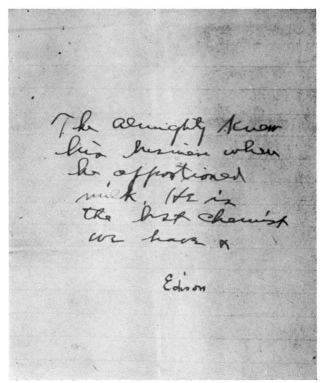

119

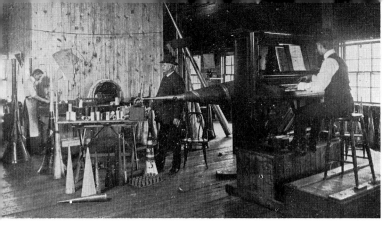

**MUSIC ROOM AT WEST ORANGE LABORATORY.** George Boehme at the piano is being recorded. A. T. E. Wangerman is in the center; Albert Kipfer is on the left. Ca. 1900. Edison National Historic Site.

**JACQUES URLUS ACCOMPANIED BY SODER'S ORCHESTRA** makes a recording in the Edison Recording Studio, 79 Fifth Ave., New York City. Ca. 1900. Edison National Historic Site.

**A CORNER OF THE CYLINDER RECORDING STUDIO.** Columbia Street, West Orange, N. J. January 22, 1917. Left to right: George Werner, Fred C. Burt. Edison National Historic Site.

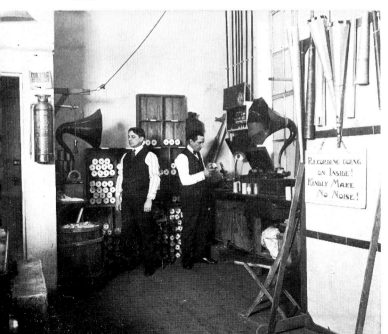

decision, and at the suggestion of Eastman, the motion picture makers agreed they would take out licenses under the Edison patent, paying a royalty of one-half cent a foot on all film they used, the Eastman Company to collect the royalty for Edison. This court decision had made it evident Edison controlled the basic patents of the motion picture industry exclusive of film. Once more he was free of debt!

In the early years of his inventing, Edison made his notes and sketches on loose sheets of paper, then pasted them in scrapbooks or stored them in large packages. Seeing the wisdom of a better system of keeping records, he adopted a uniform notebook 8½ by 6 inches of about 200 pages when he moved to Menlo Park. There are now over 2,600 such notebooks recording his countless thousands of experiments.

One of the inventor's senior staff members said, "Edison can think of more ways of doing a thing than any man I ever saw or heard of. He tries everything and never lets up, even though failure is apparently staring him in the face. He only stops when he simply can't go any further on that particular line. When he decides on any mode of procedure he gives his notes to the experimenter and lets him alone, only stepping in from time to time to look at the operations and reports of progress."

He would have no part of a reference to his "genius." "Genius," he said, "is one per cent inspiration and 99 per cent perspiration." On another occasion he stated, "Stuff! I tell you genius is hard work, stick-to-it-iveness, and common sense." E. H. Johnson, in reply, said, "Yes, I admit there is all that to it, but there is still more. Batch and I have those qualifications, but although we know quite a lot about telephones, and worked hard, we couldn't invent a brand-new non-infringing telephone receiver as you did when Gouraud cabled for one. Then, how about the subdivision of the electric light?" Edison changed the subject.

Edison compared his methods of research to those of Luther Burbank who picked one plant that showed promise out of a thousand. Edison would select one chemical experiment out of hundreds or a thousand, then pursue that one to a logical conclusion. Empirical? Yes! He admitted it but, as he said, "when it comes to problems of a mechanical nature, I want to tell you that all I've ever tackled or solved have been done by hard, logical thinking."

Always cheerful in the face of thousands of unsuccessful experiments, he once had made

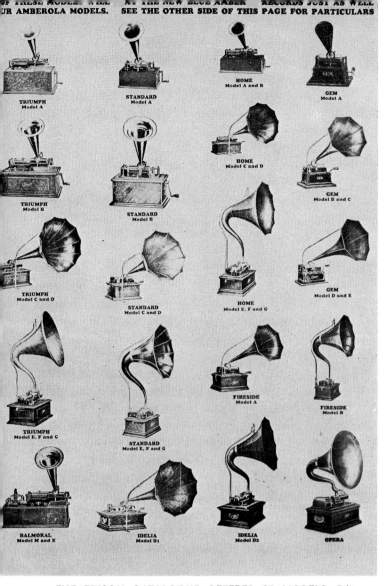

**THE EDISON CATALOGUE OFFERED 25 MODELS.** Edison National Historic Site.

**IN THE DAYS OF HOUSE CALLS.** August Strum sold black wax records and phonographs after working hours. His assistant drives the wagon. 1906-1907. Edison National Historic Site.

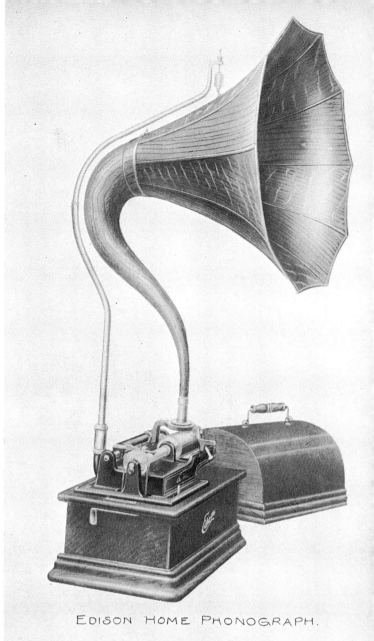

EDISON HOME PHONOGRAPH.

**EDISON HOME PHONOGRAPH WITH CYGNET HORN** was a best seller in 1911 and 1912. Edison National Historic Site.

**JOY TO THE WORLD** was an Edison by-product. Advertising chromo. Edison National Historic Site.

**Cal Stewart (Uncle Josh)**
The Edison Artist Who Has Made Millions Laugh

His philosophy is: "I'd sooner tell Peter on the Last Day about the Laffs I had given to Folks on Earth than Try to Explain to Him about Givin' them Heart Akes."

**"UNCLE JOSH,"** or Cal Stewart, was one of Edison's early recording humorists. Photo in **Edison Amberola Monthly,** October, 1919, a record dealer publication. Edison National Historic Site.

were unreliable; those run by steam were heavy and cumbersome. Battery run carriages were quiet, clean and light. Why not develop a practical battery? The electric carriage was the coming thing.

The heavy lead and sulphuric acid storage batteries were wrong in principle since they were short of life. Edison would create one that was lighter and last as long as the truck or car. After some 10,000 experiments he obtained some promising reactions between iron and nickel. Needing purer compounds of nickel hydrate and iron oxide but unable to obtain them since little was known of the quality he desired, he established a chemical plant at Silver Lake, New Jersey. The men in charge were given special training by him for the arduous tasks of search, testing and compounding.

His original idea was to use nickel hydrate for the positive pole and iron oxide for the negative pole in the form of perforated metallic pockets and tubes.

The first batteries were manufactured in 1904, at his factory in Glen Ridge, New Jersey. His sales soon exceeded the plant's ability to produce. Still, Edison was not satisfied with his product. He recognized deficiencies in it and was convinced it could be improved. A series of rigid tests convinced him the battery cells would gradually lose their capacity. Concluding that the graphite used was the cause, he made a monumental decision. He would discontinue the manufacture and sales of his battery.

The dissatisfaction with the battery was his for he had no complaints from his customers. He realized that continued sales would increase the number of defective batteries. This he did not want.

9,000 such on a new type storage battery. W. S. Mallory, a close associate, remarked that it was a shame so much work had been expended without results. With a smile Edison replied, "Results! Why man, I have gotten a lot of results! I know several thousand things that won't work!"

Edison loved speed. He was happiest on the front of a fast-moving steam locomotive or in the cab of his electric locomotive as it traveled 40 miles an hour on his Menlo Park track. Perhaps this euphoric feeling had its introduction during his period as a candy butcher in Michigan. About 1900, horseless carriages were becoming the vogue. Those run by gasoline

**HE WOULDN'T LET GO.** Edison visualized his phonograph being used in every business office as a dictation machine. 1907. Pach Bros. photo. Edison National Historic Site.

Realistically, he started on another series of experiments—some 50,000 in all—that continued over a period of five years. The end result was a remarkable battery known as the Edison Nickel-Iron Alkaline Storage Battery, production beginning on them in March, 1908. In the first year of production a million dollars' worth of the new batteries were sold. It had cost him a million dollars of his own money and then years of hard work to produce.

Edison had kept an eye on the home phonograph market. His chief competitor was the Victor Talking Machine Company for it had been producing Berliner's disc record. The disc record was easier to ship or store and was easier and less costly to reproduce. Yet Edison adhered to his celluloid cylinder, maintaining it was technically superior to the disc.

Competitive always, he began an enthusiastic program of research in the field of disc records in 1910, searching for better materials for constructing records.

From 1869—the year of his first patent — up to that summer of 1910, he had applied for 1,328 separate patents. His average was 32 for each year. In 1882, his best year, he had applied for 141 patents of which 75 were granted him.

By 1912 he was ready to make a disc record of his own. A silent, unbreakable disc with a bakelite coated surface and a diamond needle gave him a quality instrument with which his competitors found it difficult to compete. His 1914 annual phonograph business had gone over the seven million dollar mark when a tragedy struck West Orange.

Early in the evening of December 9, 1914,

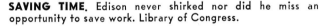

**SAVING TIME.** Edison never shirked nor did he miss an opportunity to save work. Library of Congress.

**RELAXING FOR A MOMENT.** In the center of his West Orange Laboratory library, Edison was in the center of the action. A model of his concrete house may be seen in the background. November 20, 1911. Edison National Historic Site.

a fire broke out in a film inspection booth. It was immediately out of control because of the quantities of chemicals and inflammable motion picture film stored. Six buildings were destroyed and seven others gutted. The loss of master records, raw materials, production machinery and supplies came at a time the British blockade of Germany prohibited any possiblity of replacement since the tools and chemicals were obtained from Germany. Uninsured, his loss was $5 million.

Within 36 hours the 67 year old inventor was preparing to supervise 1,500 men in constructing a new plant larger than the first. He took the challenge of a new start with a certain eagerness, even joy, saying, "No one's ever too old to make a fresh start."

Josephus Daniels, Secretary of the Navy under President Wilson, asked Edison to head a consulting board of scientists and inventors to whom all suggestions and inventions from civilians or the armed forces could go for review. Though disliking war, he accepted.

On October 21, 1915, he was the guest of honor at the Panama-Pacific Exposition in San

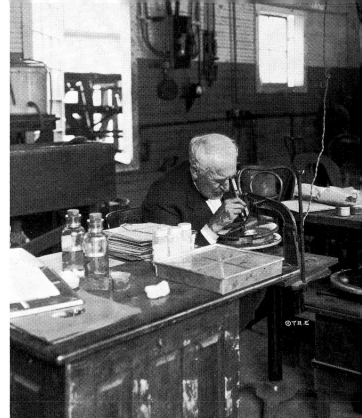

**FIRST LOVE.** Edison's first love was chemistry though his greatest accomplishments were in the field of physics. Dickson photo of Thomas A. Edison in his West Orange chemistry laboratory, December, 1890. Library of Congress.

**EXAMINING HIS DIAMOND DISC RECORDS.** The inventor never stopped his search for improvement. June 10, 1921. Edison National Historic Site.

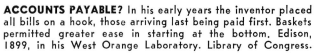

**ACCOUNTS PAYABLE?** In his early years the inventor placed all bills on a hook, those arriving last being paid first. Baskets permitted greater ease in starting at the bottom. Edison, 1899, in his West Orange Laboratory. Library of Congress.

**AN EVENING AT GLENMONT.** Edison listens to his new diamond disc phonograph. September 11, 1912. Edison National Historic Site.

Francisco on "Edison Day." Stopping at Sacramento, his special car *Superb* took on Luther Burbank, then moved on to San Francisco to be joined by Henry Ford, the three visiting Santa Rosa to view Burbank's garden. On Edison Day, the inventor was presented with a bronze medal in the overcrowded Festival Hall, with some 10,000 standing on the outside, unable to enter.

When the *U.S.S. Sussex* was torpedoed by a German U-boat on March 24, 1916, Edison and his consulting board marched in a "citizens' preparedness parade" up Fifth Avenue in New York. Threatening letters poured in but he continued with his work.

On November 12, 1920, he was awarded a Distinguished Service Medal, the only one awarded a civilian by the Navy Department. He who had detested war had contributed more than 40 inventions to aid his country.

One of his first contributions was a listening device to locate oncoming torpedoes, and a system using four sea anchors on one side of the ship so its helm could be put hard over to swing her out of harm's way. He suggested using collision mats to plug any rent in the side of a ship caused by torpedo hits.

In July 17, 1917, he responded to the call for a camouflage coloration technique. The smoke screen, or "smudging the skyline" as he called it, was his idea. He developed a high speed shutter to be used on a searchlight for using Morse code signals between ships. His list of ideas became endless, yet it appears that few were adopted. He disliked the delays and circumventions, the "red tape humbuggery" as he called it. The gold braid and naval etiquette bored him. When it was all over he declared, "I made about 45 inventions during the war, all perfectly good ones, and they pigeon-holed every one of them. Naval officers resent any interference by civilians. Those fellows are a closed corporation."

As the organizer and director of the world's first industrial research laboratory, Edison developed factory production methods and introduced quality control. It has been said he learned precision manufacturing and mass production methods from Henry Ford. Actually, he was using precision manufacturing and mass production prior to the invention of the Model T Ford.

Ford first met Edison on August 11, 1896 at a dinner at the old Manhattan Beach Hotel

**EDISON AND HIS WEST ORANGE LABORATORY STAFF.** W. K. L. Dickson photo, July 31, 1893. Left to right—First row (seated): Charles Brown, J. W. Gladstone, Thomas Maguire, John Ott, Thomas A. Edison, Charles Batchelor, W. S. Mallory, J. F. Randolph, J. W. Harris; Second row: A. Y. Stewart, W. Miller, J. W. Aylsworth, J. T. Marshall, A. E. Kennelly, P. Kenny. W. K. L. Dickson, T. Banks, H. F. Miller; Third row: S. G. Burn, Charles Wurth, F. A. Phelps Jr., F. P. Ott, E. W. Thomas, R. Lozier, William Heise, W. S. Logue, H. J. Gagan, A. T. E. Wangemann; Fourth row: L. W. Sheldon, R. Arnot, C. K. Kaiser, J. Martin, H. Reed, C. M. Dally, F. C. Devonald, A. V. Thompson. Edison National Historic Site.

**EDISON WITH HIS SON CHARLES AT GLENMONT.** 1902.
Edison National Historic Site.

several miles from Coney Island while attending an annual meeting of Edison engineers and managers. Ford, who was chief engineer of the Detroit Edison Company at the time, was attending the meeting with Alexander Dow, president of Detroit Edison.

Ford thought he had seen him earlier that year when Edison, who was returning from his father's funeral at Port Huron and staying at the Cadillac Hotel next door to Detroit Edison, walked past with a group of men and was pointed out to Ford.

Discussion at the dinner centered on the new electric horseless carriage and the use of electricity in the charging of its batteries. Alexander Dow drew attention to Ford as "a young fellow who has made a gas car." Asked how he made it go, he started to tell about it loud enough for Edison and others across the table to hear him. J. W. Lieb Jr., president of the New York Edison Company, seeing Edison cup his hand behind his ear, motioned Ford up to a seat next to Edison. Edison's questioning made it evident he had studied the gas engine.

Approving Ford's affirmative answer as to whether it was a four-cycle engine, he began a detailed series of questions on the sparking mechanism to explode gas. Ford bolstered his replies with sketches. At the conclusion Edison remarked that electric vehicles had to remain near their stations to recharge their overly heavy batteries; that steam engines had to have a boiler and fire; that Ford's car was self-

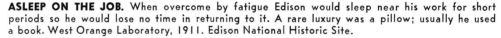

**ASLEEP ON THE JOB.** When overcome by fatigue Edison would sleep near his work for short periods so he would lose no time in returning to it. A rare luxury was a pillow; usually he used a book. West Orange Laboratory, 1911. Edison National Historic Site.

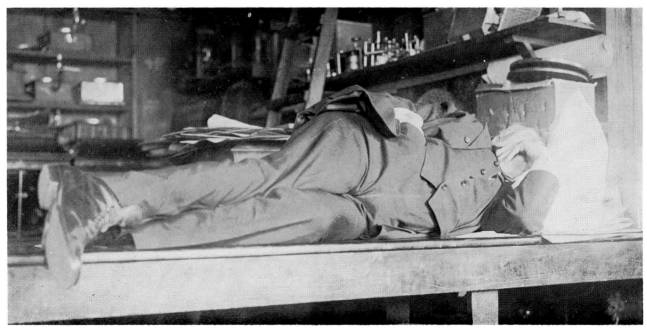

**TOO SLOW FOR THOMAS.** Mrs. Edison drove this early Baker Electric automobile that was powered by Edison storage batteries. Ca. 1903. Edison National Historic Site.

contained by carrying its own power. Bringing his fist down on the table with a bang, he concluded, "You have it! Keep at it!"

This was the first encouragement Ford had received. Coming from the world's greatest inventive genius, this approval was enough to set Ford in motion. And so a great friendship.

In February, 1914, Mr. and Mrs. Ford visited with the Edisons at Fort Myers. Joined by John Burroughs, the three men toured the Everglades. Enjoying themselves thoroughly, they promised each other they would do it again. Ford bought a winter home near Edison's Seminole Lodge.

By this time Edison was enjoying his sixth laboratory. The first of his "inventive shops" was the cellar of his Port Huron home, then came the baggage car of the Grand Trunk Railroad, followed by Newark, Menlo Park and West Orange, and now Fort Myers.

The following year, while at the 1915 Panama-Pacific Exposition, Burroughs, Edison, Ford and Harvey Firestone made an automobile tour of the countryside. So much enjoyment was derived from it they planned to take a camping trip the following summer. Such an outing became an annual event.

**THE INSOMNIA SQUAD.** September 11, 1912. Edison's assistants in his West Orange "invention factory" acquired this name because of the long periods of time they spent on some of his projects. Left to right, standing: Ed McGlynn, Bob Spahle, Archie Hoffman; Seated: Johnny LaMonte, Billy Fulton, Sam Moore, Thomas A. Edison. Edison National Historic Site.

Edison looked forward to the camping trip each year, the foursome spending as many as ten days under tents, traveling more than 2,000 miles by motor car. Edison preferred new country on each trip, the more remote and untraveled the better.

He was the most widely informed in the party for he could talk intelligently on any subject and was the only one to take any books with him, which he read at every opportunity.

Ford was the handyman of the foursome, repairing anything with little effort or equipment. Burroughs' tastes were simple. After a cup of hot water and toast, he would retire early. The rest stayed up late swapping yarns. Each had his own tent illuminated by storage batteries Edison had brought along.

Up at 6:30 A.M., Ford would use the creek to bathe, the others washing at a folding table. After breakfast prepared by a chef, they would practice shooting at a mark. Ford was the most active for he liked to explore, and he was the most adaptive. He took great interest in streams, seeing their potential in terms of water power.

Edison was the least active. He liked to sit and read or curl up and take a nap. He disliked the crowds that met them everywhere for he had gone for rest and relaxation.

When Burroughs passed away in 1921, President Warren G. Harding was taken on the next trip, stealing away from the White House to go. In 1918, on the second of the seven

**EDISON'S GOLD EXTRACTION PLANT.** Delores, New Mexico, March 18, 1900. Edison National Historic Site.

famous outings, Burroughs was 81, Edison 71, Ford was 55 and Firestone was 49.

Over the years great honors were conferred upon the venerable inventor. Perhaps the greatest was that of Henry Ford when he reconstructed Menlo Park at Greenfield Village so realistically Edison exclaimed while looking at its topsoil brought from the original Menlo Park, "Why, it's the same damned New Jersey clay!" And seated in an old chair after his first tour of the reconstruction he said to Ford, "It's ninety-nine and nine-tenths per cent perfect!" Ford wanted to know about the other one-tenth per cent. Edison replied. "Our floor was never as clean as this!"

Thomas Alva Edison had no recriminations,

**MORE TO HIS LIKING** was this touring car. August 9, 1912, in the West Orange Laboratory yard; Edison Industries building in background. Edison National Historic Site.

no regrets. His life he had lived to the fullest. He had made money, lost it, then made it again. He had people help him, steal from him, give him honors, take them away from him, yet life had been full and joyous. There was more to be done, time permitting, for he had a notebook full of ideas for the next 100 years. So he told a visitor at Fort Myers.

The sons of his first marriage had not turned out too well but his second family had been a blessing. He had a great love for his wife Mina, never leaving the house without kissing her. Their sons, Theodore and Charles, both outstanding graduates of the Massachusetts Institute of Technology, were making their mark in the world. The youngest son Theodore preferred science to business, showing great aptitude in the field of mathematics. Though heading an engineering consulting firm of his own, for a time he was technical director of the Edison Laboratory, then returned to his first love—mathematical physics.

At the age of 80 Edison turned over managerial control of Thomas A. Edison, Inc., to

**DR. JONAS W. AYLSWORTH.** As Edison's chief chemist, he played an important part in the development of the storage battery and the composition of the wax records. 1901. Edison National Historic Site.

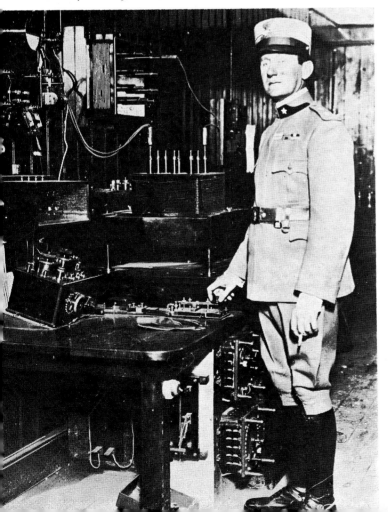

**GUGLIELMO MARCONI.** Edison admired Marconi who had purchased his patent rights to the space telegraph and aerial masts in 1904. Here Marconi is in the uniform of an Italian lieutenant while on a mission to London during World War I. Library of Congress.

his son Charles. Guiding well the fortunes of the Edison Company, Charles displayed an interest and a capacity in the field of public life. Serving under President Franklin D. Roosevelt as Assistant Secretary of the Navy and later as Secretary of the Navy, he served New Jersey as its Democratic Governor for a three-year term.

His daughter Madeleine had graduated from Bryn Mawr College, marrying John Eyre Sloane of South Orange, New Jersey, in 1914.

Now spending most of his time in his laboratory at Fort Myers, Edison was searching for a method of producing rubber from American-grown plants. Experimenting with 17,000 plants, he had found 1,200 containing enough rubber to be given further consideration, finally narrowing these down to the goldenrod. Goldenrod was selected because it was a one-season plant that could be grown anywhere in the United States and could be harvested by machinery. He estimated he could obtain 100 to 150 pounds of rubber an acre from it.

Following his collapse at the electric light Golden Jubilee at Dearborn, Michigan, in 1929, Edison had undergone a physical examination on Mrs. Edison's insistence. Digestive disturbances were discovered—gastric ulcers complicated by diabetes and Bright's disease. A diet of two glasses of milk every two hours did not prevent a relapse on August 1, 1931, but he was up and around soon after, though quite weak. From then on he spent much less time in the laboratory. He ate little, slept a great deal. Though he kept in constant touch with his technical assistants, for he wanted daily reports of the goldenrod experiment, it was Mrs. Edison who was with him constantly. By fall he knew. It would be just a matter of time —of patient waiting, but patience always had been his principal virtue.

On October 18, 1931, the lights went out for Thomas Alva Edison.

**A REPORTER TELLS A STORY TO EDISON.** 1906. Byron photo, N. Y. Library of Congress.

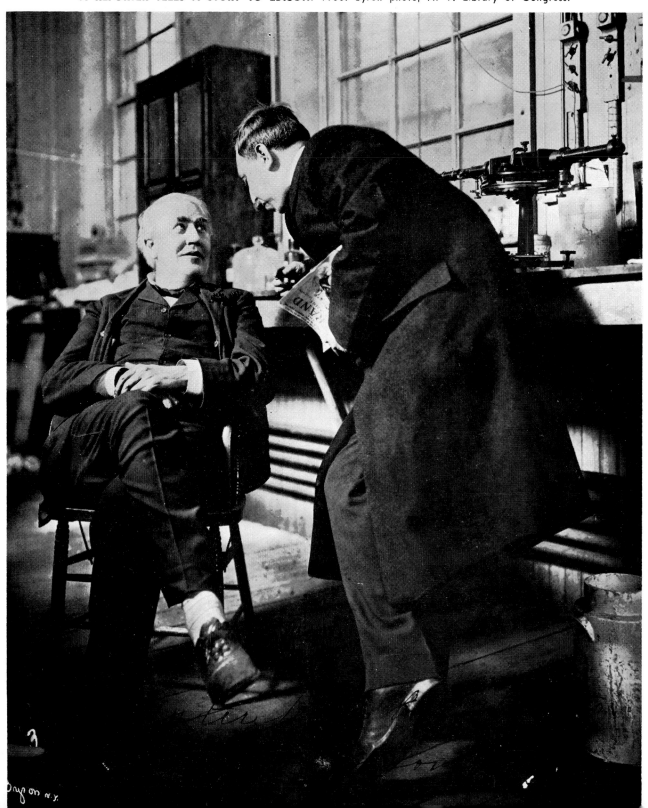

**EDISON TELLS HIS STORY TO THE REPORTER.** 1906. Byron photo, N. Y. Library of Congress.

**ALWAYS A CHEMIST.** Edison loved his chemicals. 1906. Byron photo, N.Y. Edison National Historic Site.

**FIRST LARGE CURTIS STEAM TURBINE GENERATOR.** Returned to Schenectady in 1909 for preservation. Left to right: E. W. Rice Jr., W. L. R. Emmet, Thomas A Edison, George F. Morrison, Charles P. Steinmetz, H. F. T. Erben. Used by permission of the General Electric Company.

**MR. AND MRS. THOMAS A. EDISON IN THE WEST ORANGE CHEMISTRY LABORATORY.** 1906. Byron photo, N.Y. Edison National Historic Site.

**FISHING AT FT MYERS, FLORIDA.** It is told that Edison would fish for hours without any bait on his hook. No assistant would dare scare the fish away by the shouting necessary to convey a message to him. And no fish would disturb a baitless hook. In this manner he was able to meditate for hours without being disturbed. Ca. 1909. Edison National Historic Site.

**THE EDISON FAMILY IN BERLIN, GERMANY.** Taken in the Hotel Ublon, September 26, 1911. Charles is not in the picture. Edison National Hisoric Site.

**A BAILEY AUTOMOBILE CALLED "MAUD."** The car was manufactured by the S. R. Bailey Co. Inc., Amesburg, Mass. The man behind the wheel is Captain George W. Langdon, test driver for S. R. Bailey Co. To the left is Frank McGinness, an Edison Company engineer. Thomas A. Edison leans on a front mudguard. 1910. Edison National Historic Site.

**A DETROIT ELECTRIC AUTOMOBILE IN THE WEST ORANGE LABORATORY YARD.** Edison is seated on the left; other man unidentified. Ca. 1911. Edison National Historic Site. picture. Edison National Historic Site.

**FRED OTT WORKING ON A BENZOL EXPERIMENT.** January 11, 1915. Edison National Historic Site.

**EDISON FIELD DAY AT OLYMPIC PARK.** Edison throws a baseball to start the game. August 12, 1912. Edison National Historic Site.

**THE EDISONS IN THEIR ELECTRIC RUNABOUT.** 1914. Library of Congress.

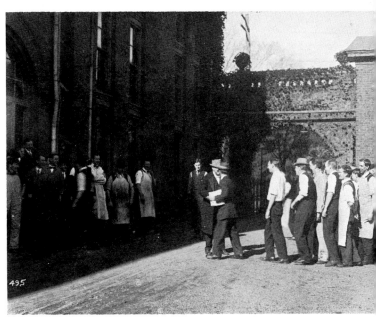

**WELCOME HOME.** Edison's reward on his return from Europe is a yard full of smiling faces at the West Orange Laboratory. October 9, 1911. Edison National Historic Site.

**STARTING A RACE ON EDISON FIELD DAY.** This was an annual event sponsored by his employees in his honor. 1913. Library of Congress.

**STORAGE BATTERY ASSEMBLY DEPARTMENT.** Lakeside Avenue battery plant at West Orange, N.J. Edison's durable alkaline storage batteries were the result of years of research and a million dollars of expense. January 14, 1915. Edison National Historic Site.

**MR. EDISON CHECKS PROGRESS IN THE MACHINE SHOP.** West Orange Laboratory, 1915. Library of Congress.

**EDISON RUNS A TEST.** He observes while a typist uses his dictation machine. July 20, 1914. Edison National Historic Site.

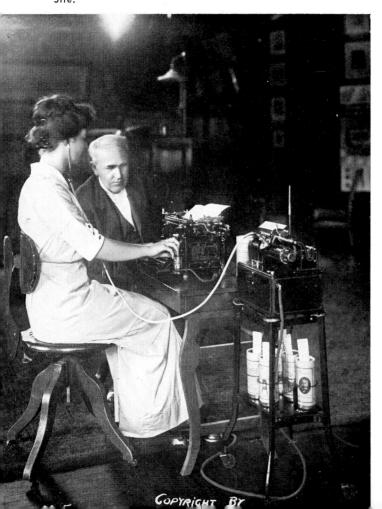

**INSPECTING EDISON'S ALKALINE STORAGE BATTERIES FOR SUBMARINES.** Edison (center) developed a battery that reduced danger of noxious gas when the submarine was submerged. August 21, 1915. Left to right: Mr. Bachman, T. A. Edison, Miller Reese Hutchson. Edison National Historic Site.

**DISTINGUISHED GUESTS.** A continuous stream of visitors, many of them distinguished, came to the West Orange Laboratories to visit the inventor. Left to right, front row: Ambassabor (to Great Britain) Joseph H. Choate, Mrs. T. A. Edison, Mrs. Choate, T. A. Edison May 26, 1915. Edison National Historic Site.

**A VISIT WITH LUTHER BURBANK.** Luther Burbank is at left with hat and coat on his arm; Edison has a rose in his buttonhole. Edison admired the botanist, pointing out that their methods of experimentation were similar. Santa Rosa, California, home of Burbank. 1915. Edison National Historic Site.

**ATTENDING THE PANAMA-PACIFIC EXPOSITION.** Left to right: Henry Ford, Thomas A. Edison, Luther Burbank, Harvey Firestone Sr., 1915. Hartsook photo, San Francisco. Firestone Tire & Rubber Company.

**EDISON AND EVANGELIST BILLY SUNDAY.** Ca. 1915. Edison National Historic Site.

**A CONSULTATION.** Outside the door to the West Orange Laboratory. August 9, 1915. Left to right: M. R. Hutchison, Edward Marshall, T. A. Edison, Hudson Maxim. Edison National Historic Site.

**A U. S. NAVY CONSULTING BOARD** was appointed during World War I by Secretary of the Navy Josephus Daniels to review all ideas and suggestions offered by civilian or service inventors to determine if they were practical and usable. Standing on bottom step, left to right: Frank J. Sprague, L. H. Baekeland, M. R. Hutchison, Thomas A. Edison (chairman), Josephus Daniels, Franklin D. Roosevelt (Assistant Secretary of the Navy) 1915. Edison National Historic Site.

**EDISON STORAGE BATTERY COMPANY SEARCHLIGHT** is shown on the Valley Road (now Main Stret) mounted on a Model T Ford, across from the West Orange Laboratory. November 3, 1915. Edison National Historic Site.

**EDISON AND THE NAVY CONSULTING BOARD, WORLD WAR I.** Front row, left to right: Franklin D. Roosevelt, Hiram Maxim, Thomas A. Edison, Secretary of Navy Josephus Daniels, others unidentified. 1915. Edison National Historic Site.

**EDISON MEETS REAR ADMIRAL WILLIAM F. FULTON ON THE U. S. S. OREGON.** Officer to the right is Joseph F. Reeves. Edison National Historic Site.

**TALKING TO A BODYGUARD.** A valuable asset, Edison was guarded during World War I. 1915. Edison National Historic Site.

**INSPECTING A SUBMARINE.** Edison boards the U.S.S. E-2 to look over his storage battery installation. December, 1915. Edison National Historic Site.

**A MESSAGE FROM THE OLD MAN.** When a group of old telegraphers visited Edison at West Orange, he rigged up a telegraph key to an automobile horn to get his message to them. Left to right, M. R. Hutchison, Edison, Mrs. Edison, William H. Meadowcroft. September 27, 1916. Edison National Historic Site.

**MILLER REESE HUTCHISON** was Edison's special assistant and a member of the Navy Consulting Board. Edison National Historic Site.

**LOOKING THINGS OVER.** Edison took his appointment to the Navy Consulting Board seriously. Though he disliked war he contributed over 40 inventions to aid his country. 1915. Edison National Historic Site.

**ABOARD SHIP.** Secretary of War Josephus Daniels is in the front center with Mr. Edison on his right. 1918. Edison National Historic Site.

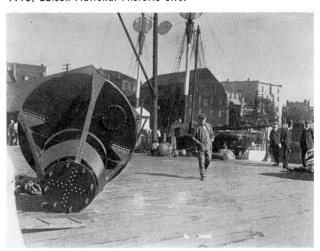

**EDISON IN HIS LIBRARY** inspects a diamond disc record. Pach Bros. photo, September 20, 1916. Edison National Historic Site.

**VISITORS FROM FRANCE.** A commission of French scientists and military men visited the West Orange Laboratories July 13, 1917. Edison National Historic Site.

**TWO WHITE STEAMERS IN DISTRESS.** Edison led a prospecting party—consisting of his son Charles, J. V. Miller, George Poppa, Fred Ott and a prospector—from West Orange down into North Carolina on a search for cobalt to be used in his storage batteries. Transportation problems were so frequent the White Steamers were named "Discord" and "Disaster." Left to right: Edison, sleeping, George Poppa, Fred Ott. J. V. Miller photo, May 24, 1906. Edison National Historic Site.

**ROADSIDE BREAKFAST.** Edison in shirt-sleeves and cap; George Poppa in galluses on his left.. J. V. Miller photo, May, 1906. Edison National Historic Site.

**ROAD BLOCK.** Though they had their troubles, the Edison party found cobalt 10 miles east of Lincolnton, N.C. May 27, 1906. J. V. Miller photo. Edison National Historic Site.

*From the Laboratory of Thomas A. Edison, Orange. N.J. Aug 14*

Dear Canty

In reply to your question, let me say that I was the first person to speak into the first phonograph. The first words spoken by me into the original model, and that were reproduced, were "Mary had a little lamb" and the other three lines of that verse.

Yours sincerely

Thos A Edison

**EDISON'S REPLY** to a question about the tinfoil phonograph. August 14, 1918. Edison National Historic Site.

**REAR END TROUBLE AGAIN.** The cobalt prospecting trip took from May 16 to June 15, 1906, the two White Steamers being shipped back from Sylva, N.C. The party traveled 2,500 miles, 1,171 miles of it by automobile. J. V. Miller photo. Edison National Historic Site.

**AT HOME IN FLORIDA.** left to right: T. A. Edison, John Burroughs, Henry Ford—at Ft. Myers, Fla. 1914. Courtesy T. A. Edison Home, Ft. Myers, Fla.

**HENRY FORD, THOMAS EDISON, HARVEY S. FIRESTONE.** Ca. 1915. Firestone Tire & Rubber Company.

**THEN THERE WERE THREE.** Left to right: Henry Ford, Thomas Edison, Harvey S. Firestone at a lumber camp in Sidnaw, Michigan, August 22, 1923, while on their annual camping trip. Firestone Tire & Rubber Company.

**CAMPERS FOR 1923.** Left to right: Henry Ford, Thomas Edison, Harvey S. Firestone. August, 1923. Firestone Tire & Rubber Company.

**A WELCOME TO VERMONT.** When the famous summer campers visited Vermont, President Calvin Coolidge invited them to his home on August 19, 1924, where he presented them with a sap bucket that had been in his family for many generations. Left to right: Harvey S. Firestone, President Coolidge, Henry Ford, Thomas A. Edison, Mrs. Coolidge, Russell A. Firestone and the President's father, Colonel John Coolidge. Firestone Tire & Rubber Company.

**CROWN PRINCE OF SWEDEN VISITS EDISON AT GLEN-MONT.** June 2, 1926. Edison National Historic Site.

**PROUD GRANDFATHER.** Seated with Edison are his daughter Madeleine's children, Ted, Jack and Peter Sloane. August 21, 1926. Charles James Fox photo, Orange, N.J. Library of Congress.

**WITH A ROSE IN HIS LAPEL.** In front of the Firestone residence in 1928. Library of Congress.

**A PAGE FROM HIS BOOK.** Page 85, written when Edison was 81, shows a sturdy, readable hand throughout. Edison's complete interest in his experiment is evident in the accompanying photograph made while he was writing. Notes were written on November 5, 1928. (see center of page 150) Edison National Historic Site.

**SPEAKING FROM HIS LIBRARY TO SCHENECTADY, N. Y.**
Charles Edison listens to his father as the broadcast begins.
Ca. 1930. Edison National Historic Site.

**A CREATURE OF HABIT.** A candid photograph of complete
concentration while writing in one of his 2,500 notebooks.
November 5, 1928. Edison National Historic Site.

**NO MIKE FRIGHT AT THE AGE OF 82.** Speaking before a
microphone on his birthday, February 11, 1929. Edison National Historic Site.

**START OF A CAMPING TRIP.** Left to right: Edward H. Hurley, World War I Shipping Commissioner; naturalist John Burroughs, T. A. Edison, Henry Ford, Harvey Firestone, Professor R. J. H. DeLoach. Photo presumed to have been taken at Pittsburgh, August 18, 1918. Edison National Historic Site.

**VISITING AN OLD GRIST MILL.** In the West Virginia mountains, August 21, 1918. Left to right: Thomas A. Edison, Harvey S. Firestone Jr., John Burroughs, Henry Ford, Harvey S. Firestone; seated below, R. J. H. DeLoach. Firestone Tire & Rubber Company.

**THE GYPSIES RUN A LOGGING ENGINE** at Horseshoe Run Camp, August 21, 1918. Firestone Tire & Rubber Company.

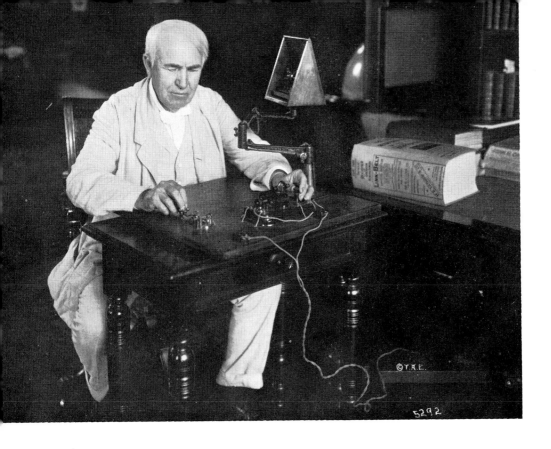

**ALWAYS THE TELEGRAPHER.** Edison never lost his touch, enjoying moments when he could put his fingers to the telegraph key. July 7, 1920. Edison National Historic Site.

**OLD TIME TELEGRAPHERS GIVE A BIRTHDAY PARTY.** Left to right: Mr. and Mrs. T. A. Edison, Mr. and Mrs. Charles Edison, Thomas A. Edison Jr. Febuary 11, 1920. Library of West Orange Laboratories. Edison National Historic Site.

**ONE DAY WONDER.** An Edison all-concrete house that was completely poured in one day. Completed house is on the right. Union, N.J., October 9, 1919. Edison National His-

**BIRTHDAY GIFT IN 1922.** His friends knew what he would enjoy the most—a Paragon radio. February 11, 1922. Lueder photo. Edison National Historic Site.

**PUNCHING THE TIME CLOCK.** Edison is shown punching the clock on his 74th birthday, a part of his daily routine at the West Orange Laboratories. A sign on the clock indicated that cigarette smoking was forbidden. February 11, 1921. Lueder photo. Edison National Historic Site.

**SUMMER CAMP NEAR HAGERSTOWN, MARYLAND.** On July 23, 1921, President Warren G. Harding joined the gypsy vacationers. Left to right: Henry Ford, Thomas A. Edison, President Harding, Harvey S. Firestone. Firestone Tire & Rubber Company.

**NOSTALGIA REPAIRED.** Edison visited his birthplace in Milan, Ohio, August 11, 1923. This residence is open to the public the year around, and is maintained by the Edison Birthplace Association Inc. C. S. Bateham photo, Norwalk, O. Ohio Historical Society Library.

**A LAMP THAT SAVED LIVES.** On October 13, 1914, the inventor obtained a patent on this electric safety lantern which greatly reduced mine accidents formerly caused by old-fashioned open flame miners' lamps. May, 1923. Lueder photo. Edison National Historic Site.

**TWO GENIUSES.** Thomas Edison and Charles P. Steinmetz at the General Electric Company, Schenectady, N.Y., October 18, 1922. Acme photo. Edison National Historic Site.

**A REAR VIEW OF THE EDISON BIRTHPLACE IN MILAN, OHIO,** (1947) indicates that the Edisons were above average means. This back yard continues down to the old Milan Canal. Courtesy of Mr. Edison's daughter, Mrs. John Eyre Sloane.

**MOMENTS OF RELAXATION.** Edison reads on the front lawn of his Glenmont home. June 30, 1917. Edison National Historic Site.

# Portraits Of The Wonderous Wizard Of Menlo Park

Much of today's prosperity is based on Edison's inventions in the field of lighting, power and communications. He provided us with: unlimited daylight (incandescent light); a dynamo that converted 90% of its power into electricity as compared to the previous 40%; a three-wire system of electrical distribution so that electricity would not be a luxury for the few; motors for use on every tool instead of cumbersome leather belts, thereby lowering costs by increasing efficiency and production; a new method of mixing concrete for economy in construction; a process of extracting iron from lowgrade ore; and an improved typewriter for commercial use, to name a very few. Joe Wheelan photo taken at Glenmont in 1931, the last to be taken of Thomas Alva Edison. Edison National Historic Site.

Sketch made of Edison in Europe by Groffer. September 24, 1911. Edison National Historic Site.

**RELAXATION AT FT. MYERS, FLORIDA.** Ca 1909. Edison National Historic Site.

Edison and his associates were involved in legal strife most of his last 40 years in an effort to protect his numerous inventions. Litigation continued almost day to day because of the many infringers. 1930. Edison National Historic Site.

Henry Ford first met Edison on August 11, 1896, at the old Manhattan Beach Hotel several miles from Coney Island. A firm and close friendship followed. Many years later Ford recalled that, "He (Edison) was the first man ever to help me." Ca. 1896. Edison National Historic Site.

**ASSEMBLY AT DEARBORN, MICHIGAN.** On the morning of October 21, 1929, President Hoover arrived in Dearborn as the head of a delegation of the nation's most eminent and distinguished scientists, politicians, financiers and industrialists to pay homage to an invention that changed the world. It was the 50th anniversary of the incandescent lamp. Left to right: Henry Ford, engineer, Mrs. T. A. Edison, Mr. Edison, President Hoover. October 21, 1929. Edison National Historic Site.

**RE-ENACTMENT.** Edison, in the presence of Henry Ford and his old assistant Francis Jehl, reenacts the making of his incandescent lamp. The scene took place on the second floor of his reconstructed Menlo Park laboratory at Dearborn in the presence of many notables. October 21, 1929. Edison National Historic Site.

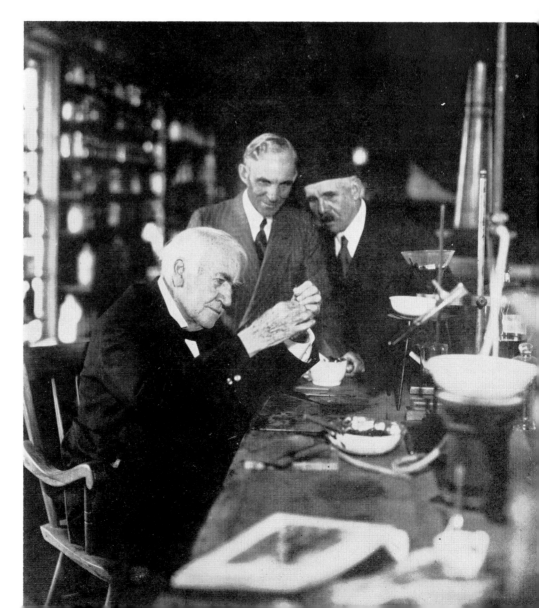

**FT. MYERS LABORATORY.** The search for cheaper rubber. Ca. 1930. Courtesy T. A. Edison Home, Ft. Myers, Fla.

**BIRTHDAY VISITORS.** At Edison's Ft. Myers home on his 82nd birthday were, left to right: Herbert Hoover, Henry Ford, Edison, Harvey S. Firestone. February 11, 1929. Edison National Historic Site.

**DIRECTING RESEARCH.** George Hart at work in the Chemical Laboratory with Edison a close observer. December 3, 1929. Edison National Historic Site.

**GOLDENROD GARDENER.** The high cost of rubber in 1924-1925 caused Edison to organize the Edison Botanic Research Company in 1927 for the express purpose of discovering a domestic source for rubber. He conducted his studies at Ft. Myers. Examining over 14,000 plants, he concentrated upon goldenrod since it yielded about five per cent rubber. He stands in his goldenrod garden at Ft. Myers. Ca 1927-1928. Edison National Historic Site.

**OLD CRONIES.** Henry Ford (left) and Edison (center) and Harvey Firestone go over a problem in the Fort Myers chemistry laboratory in 1931. Library of Congress.

**THE LAST PORTRAIT OF EDI-SON** was painted by Lucius W. Hitchcock, artist, in early 1931 at Glenmont. June 30, 1931. Edison National Historic Site.

**MRS. THOMAS ALVA EDISON IN 1947.** Edison National Historic Site.

**IN HIS WEST ORANGE LABORATORY.** Here too he searched for a cheap rubber supply. 1930. Edison National Historic Site.

In good general health at the age of 63, and very active, he never took systematic exercise. Weighing 175 pounds, he ate pretty much what he liked. He was fond of fruit but cared little for meat. He seldom used alcohol but liked strong coffee, cigars and chewing tobacco, despising cigarettes. 1911. Edison National Historic Site.

He might sleep four hours or nine hours or not sleep at all, depending upon his need. When deeply engrossed in something he would keep at it until his mind ceased to function. When he arrived at that point he would lie down right there and go to sleep. March 12, 1911. Edison National Historic Site.

**OPPOSITE**—The inventor always dressed quite plainly for he had no interest in clothes. He ordered suits from measurements made 20 years prior since there had been little physical change. Pach Bros. photo. 1906. Edison National Historic Site.

It was his opinion that time in school was wasted on subjects not essential. The only college graduates he had any liking for were those from an institute of technology. He contended that the country needed the practical, skilled engineer who could do anything—that there would be a time for literary men in three or four centuries. 1913. Edison National Historic Site.

In an argument he was vehement in making a point. When he laughed he shouted with glee, rocking back and forth and slapping his hands on his knees. Engraving by E. G. Williams & Bros., New York. Ohio Historical Society Library.

"You (Edison) have been equally successful as a pioneer, executive and organizer. Your construction of the electric lamp has to a great extent made the development of a great electrical industry possible. The great technical creators, of which you are one of the most successful, have produced in the course of a century an entirely new situation to which mankind has not yet adapted himself." Albert Einstein. Ca. 1927-1928. Courtesy of T. A. Edison Home, Ft. Myers, Fla.

Henry Ford was of the opinion that Edison had created millions of new jobs, made jobs more remunerative, and had done more to abolish poverty than all of the politicians, statesmen and reformers put together. February 11, 1920 (73rd birthday). Edison National Historic Site.

Edison rarely gave verbal instructions, finding it easier and quicker to write or draw his instructions than to talk. His writing was very readable and his sketches quite clear. Thus he kept a running record of every experiment. A number of investigations were carried on at the same time, frequently unrelated. Portrait by Sylvette. 1925. Edison National Historic Site.

His very first invention was a device he thought was needed. When he discovered it wasn't wanted he determined to concentrate on inventing things he knew were wanted. From that point on he took nothing for granted. Walter Scott Shinn photo. May 13, 1919. Edison National Historic Site.

He usually wore summer suits the year around. In the coldest weather he would vary the number of underclothing, wearing three or four if the cold weather warranted it. 1931. Courtesy T. A. Edison Home, Ft. Myers, Florida.

Notion Books or Day Books, as Edison called them were used to record his daily experiments. He dated each page and had the date attested to by three witnesses. Each illustration, formula and important paragraph was initialled so there would be ample evidence in the event of law suits. He frequently made comments or notations as: NG for No Good, LB for Little Better, DB for Damn Bad, E for Encouraging, VE for Very Encouraging, and "Eureka!" when he obtained a success. 1926. Edison National Historic Site.

**OPPOSITE**—The inventor compared his methods of research to those of Luther Burbank who picked one plant that showed promise out of a thousand. Edison would select one chemical experiment out of hundreds or thousands then pursue it to a logical conclusion. Winemiller and Miller photo. Spring, 1925. Edison National Historic Site.

# Medals Presented To Thomas Alva Edison

**MEDALS PRESENTED TO THOMAS ALVA EDISON.** 1. Silver medal making him a chevalier of the French Legion of Honor, November 15, 1878. Ob: Honeur et Patrie; Re: Republique Francaise, 1870. 2. Gold medal making him an officer of the French Legion of Honor, 1881. Same inscription as #1. 3. Gold medal from the French Legion of Honor bestowing its highest award—the title of commander, 1889. Same inscription. 4. Gold medal from King Humbert of Italy making Edison a Grand Officer of the Crown of Italy with the title of "Count." August, 1889. Mounted on a ribbon to wear around his neck. 5. Same as #4 but mounted on an eight-point silver star pin. 6. Gold medal Ob: Republique Francaise; Re: Exposition Universelle International de 1878. Edison, Paris. 7. Silver medal—Ob: Science, Industry; Re: Crystal Palace Electrical Exposition, 1892. 8. Gold medal—Ob: Thomas Alva Edison; Re: New Grand Central Palace, New York, Oct. 15-25, 1913. The Electrical Exposition and Motorshow of 1913. 9. Gold medal—Ob: Societa Delle Scienze; Re: Premio Matteucci. Thomas Alva Edison—1887. 10. Bronze French medal—Ob: Inventon de la Photographic Nicephore-Niepoe-L. J. Daguerre; Re: Divulgation de la Photographie 1839-Cinquantenaire-1889, Thomas A. Edison (Etats-Unis). 11. Congressional Medal received from Secretary of the Treasurey Andrew Melon on October 20, 1928; Ob: Edison. 1928, Re: Medal of the Congress of the United States. He illuminated the Path of Progress by His Inventions. 12. Bronze medal-Ob: In honor of the guests who attended the dedicatory ceremonies on the opening of the building of the Chamber of Commerce; Re: To commemorate the opening of the building of the Chamber of Commerce of the State of New York, November 11, 1902. 13. Gold medal-Ob: Founded 1795, Inc. 1806; Re: The Mass. Charitable Mechanic Association Award to Thomas A. Edison for Transmitter.—1878. 14. Silver Italian medal—Ob: Alexandre Votae Novocomensi, V. C.; Re: Areanis Naturae Detectis, Simulacrum in Fovo Patriae Dedicatum An-M-MDCCCXX-XVIII (1838). 15. Medal from Panama Pacific International Exposition—Ob: Replique Francaise: Re: Mr. and Mrs. Thomas Edison visited the French Pavilion at the P. P. I. E., Oct. 25, 1915. 16. Silver medal—Ob: Melbourne International Exhibition MDCCLXXX (1880); Re: "Vitam Excalvere Per Artes"; Edge: Thomas A. Edison—Electric Pen. 17. Ob: The John Fritz Medal. MCMII; Re: 1908. Awarded to Thomas Alva Edison. For Scientific or Industrial Achievement. 18. Swedish Royal Academy of Science medal—Ob: Claes-Adolf-Adelskold—1907; Re: Kungl-Svenska-Vetenskapsakadademien T. A. Edison. Phonografens, och den Elektriska Goldampans Uppfinnare. 19. Bronze medal—Ob: Republique Francaise. Th. A. Edison; Re: Exposition Universelle—1889. 20. Gold medal—Ob: Science. Industry: Re: Crystal Palace International Exposition—1882; Edge: T. A. Edison, for complete system of lighting and other exhibits. 21. Bronze medal—Ob: American Institute, New York; Re: Medal of Excellence. Awarded to Thos. Alva Edison for duplicating ink.—1878. 22. Bronze medal for electric pen—Ob: International Exhibition, Sidney, N. S. W. MDCCCLXXIX (1879); Re: Professor Edison. First Award. 23. Silver cigar holder from Czar of Russia for Edison's gift of the phonograph. 7/19/1889. 24. Emil Rathenau medal presented January 24, 1813, by National Safety Council for invention of Miner's Safety Cap Lamp. Ob: Emil Rathenau LXX-IAHRE-ALT-XI-DEZ-MCMVIII: Re: TREVE A-E-G-B-E-W-FVER-VERDENST-UND. 25. Gold medal—Ob: Benjamin Count Rumford Born 1753, Died 1814; Re: Rumford Medal for discoveries in light or heat. Awarded by the American Academy of Arts and Sciences to Thomas Alva Edison for his investigations in electric lighting—1895. 26. Gold English medal—Ob: Albert Prince Consort President 1842-61; Re: Society of Arts Manufactures and Commerce MDCCCLXII. 27. Bronze medal—Ob: Souvenir de Mon Ascension au Sommet de la tour Eiffel 10 September, 1889; Re: Les Travaux ent commerce, le 27 Janv. 1887 Le Monument Aete Inaugure, le 6 Mai, 1889.

28. Bronze medal—Ob: DIVINE DISIVNCTA IVNXIT HOMO; Re: Panama Pacific International Exposition, San Francisco. MCMXV (1915). Medal of Award. 29. Bronze plaque—Ob: Society of Arts and Sciences. Edison Tribute. May 24th, 1918. 30. Gold medal—Ob: American Dahlia Society in New York, Organized May 10th, 1915; Re: Awarded to Thomas A. Edison in appreciation of his great service to humanity. 31. Gold medal from Pope Pius XI—Ob: Pius XI Pent-Max-An I; Re: A-CIVITATE-VATICANA-CONDITA. ANNO I. 32. Bronze medal—Ob: American Institute of New York; Re: The Medal of Superiority awarded to Thomas A. Edison for an Electric Pen. 1878. 33. Bronze medal—Ob: International Assembly, Detroit, Mich. Oct. 21, 1929. Thomas A. Edison; Re: Presented to Thomas Alva Edison by the Inter-state Post Graduate Medical Association of North America, to commemorate his contribution to the progress of scientific medicine and his benefactions to humanity. 34. Bronze medal—Ob: Women's Roosevelt Memorial Association Service; Re: Theodore Roosevelt. Born October 27, 1958. Died, January 6, 1919. 35. Silver medal—Ob: Thomas Alva Edison MDCCCCV. Awarded by the American Institute of Electrical Engineers for meritorius achievement in electricity, 1923. 36. Gold medal —Ob: Universal Exposition, Saint Louis, United States of America. MCMIV (1904); Re: Gold Medal. Louisiana Purchase Exposition. 37. Bronze medal—Ob: Thomas A. Edison; Re: 1877-1917. To Thomas A. Edison from the National distributing and service organizations. Celebrating forty years of progress of Edison Dictating Machines. August 12, 1917. 38. Bronze medal—Ob: Massachusetts Institute of Technology MCMXVI (1916); Re: In memory of its founder William Barton Rogers. An alumni tribute at the dedication of the new buildings. 39. Gold medal—Ob: Society of Arts and Sciences. Awarded to Thomas A. Edison. May 24, 1928; Re: Science. 40. Identical to #25, except medal is silver instead of gold. 41. Bronze replica of the United States Congressional Medal. 42. Bronze wall plaque—Ob: T. A. Edison, Menlo Park. 43. Gold medal Ob: Comite de Homenaje. Thomas Alva Edison; Re: 1879-1929. Association—Argentina de Electrotecnices Invencion de la Lampara-Incabdescente. 44. Bronze medal—Thomas A. Edison; Re: Commemorating the fiftieth anniversary of the invention of the incandescent lamp by Thomas A. Edison at Menlo Park, State of New Jersey. Fine Arts Department of the Whitehead and Hoag Co., at Newark, N.J. 45. Copper medal—Ob: awarded by the City of Philadelphia; Re: The John Scott Medal—To the most Deserving. Thomas A. Edison, The greatest inventor of this or any other age. December 11, 1929. 46. Silver medal—Ob: Allessandro Volta; Re: I Centenario Voltiane Como 1827-1927.

47. Medal presented by the United States Field Artillery. 48. Silver fob—Ob: Thomas A. Edison; Re: Dinner tendered to Thomas A. Edison on his seventieth birthday by his employees at Orange, New Jersey (1917). 49. Gold medal—Presented November 12, 1920—Ob: United States of America—Navy; Re: For Distinguished Service. 50. Silver pin—Ob: D A T V 1910. 51. Gold medal—Ob: Light's Golden Jubilee. Thomas A. Edison; Re: Dedicated to better vision. 1879. 1929. 52. Gold medal—Ob: Instrucion Publica; Re: La Republica de Venezuela honra a los Colaboradores de la Instruccion Publica. 53. Gold lapel button—Edison's attendance badge at Institute of Electrical Engineers of Japan. 54. Gold medal—(Siam?). 55. Gold watch fob—Ob: Edison Electric Illuminating Co. of New York; Re: Thomas A. Edison, Director. $10 reward for return to Co. 56. Silver medal—Ob: Hudson-Fulton Celebration, N.Y.; Re: Henry Hudson 1609, Hebert Fulton 1807, 1909. 57. Gold medal—Ob: Montclair Academy Chess and Checker Club. 1915. 58. Gold medal—On bar with pin: Newark—The inventive and industrial center of the United States. Seth Boyden; On circular medal: Extends welcome to the Honorary Commercial Commissioners of Japan. Oct. 27, 1909; On pendant shield: Commerce and Navigation. 59. Gold medal—Ob: L'Academie Internationale de Geographie, Botanique, a la Science; Re: Deo Scientiarum Domine Laus et Gloria. 60. Gold medal—Ob: Civitan (Civitan Club of Florida). 61. Gold fob—Re: Disc from Allesandre Volta's first pile, injured in fire destroying the Volta Centennial Exp. at Domo, Italy, 1900. Presented to Thomas Alva Edison on his 74th birthday, Feb. 11, 1921, by William J. Hammer, President of the Edison Pioneers, 1920-21, who secured same from the custodian of the Volta relics at Como, Italy. Volta invented the electric pile, electric battery, the condenser, electrophorus, radiometer, electroscope, hydrogen lamp, etc. 62. Silver theatre pass—Ob: To the manager of any Universal Theatre in the World. Pass Thomas A. Edison and Party. Dated Feb. 11, 1928. Carl Lemmels. 63. Bronze plaque—Ob: AAN DE PIONEERS DER ELECTROTECHNIEK IN NEDERLAND AANGEBODEN DOOR HET EDISON LIGHTWEEK COMITE; Re: AAN THOMAS ALVA EDISON. 64. Bronze plaque—Same as #42. 65. Bronze plaque—Ob: Association of Edison Illuminating Companies 44th Annual Meeting. Old Point Comfort. Oct. 1-5, 1928. Iron from plating of Ironclad Merrimac. 1862.

# Bibliography

Ackerman, Carl W. *George Eastman.* New York, 1930.

Ames, Edward C. *Beyond Wonder And Discovery.* Detroit, 1967.

Ballentine, Caroline F. "The True Story of Edison's Childhood and Boyhood." *Michigan History Magazine,* Vol. 4 (1920).

Bancroft, William L. "A History of the Military Reservation at Fort Gratiot, With Reminiscences of Some of the Officers Stationed There." *Historical Collections of Michigan,* Vol. XI (1908).

Beasley, Rex. *Edison.* New York, 1964.

Bernhardt, Sarah. *Memories of My Life.* New York, 1907.

Bowen, Harold G. *The Edison Effect.* West Orange, N. J., 1951.

Bradford, Gamaliel. *The Quick And The Dead.* New York, 1931.

Bryan, George S. *Edison; The Man And His Work.* New York, 1926.

Carlson, Oliver. *The Man Who Made News: James Gordon Bennett.* New York, 1942.

Coe, Douglas. *Marconi: Pioneer of Radio.* New York, 1943.

Collins, Frederick L. *Consolidated Gas Company of New York.* New York, 1934.

Crowther, James G. *Famous American Men of Science.* New York, 1937.

.................................... *Six Great Inventors.* London, 1954.

Cullum, George W. *Biographical Register of the Officers and Graduates of the U. S. Military Academy.* 3 vols. New York, 1891.

Daly, Robert. *The World Beneath The City.* New York, 1959.

Daniels, Josephus. *The Wilson Era: Years of War And After, 1917-1923.* Chapel Hill, N. C., 1946.

.................................... *The Wilson Era: Years of Peace, 1910-1917.* Chapel Hill, N. C., 1944.

Dickson, W. K. L. and Antonia. *The Life And Inventions of Thomas Alva Edison.* New York, 1894.

Dyer, Frank L. and Martin, Thomas C. *Edison, His Life And Inventions.* 2 vols. New York, 1910.

Fanning, Leonard M. *Fathers of Industries.* New York, 1962.

Firestone, Harvey S. and Crowther, Samuel. *Men And Rubber.* New York, 1926.

Fleming, J. A. *Fifty Years of Electricity.* London, 1921.

Ford, Henry. *Edison As I Knew Him.* New York, 1930.

Gelatt, Roland. *The Fabulous Phonograph.* New York, 1955.

Greusel, J. H. *Thomas A. Edison, The Man, His Work, His Mind.* Los Angeles, 1913.

Grigg, E. R. N. *The Trail of the Invisible Light.* Springfield, Ill., 1965.

Hammond, John W. *Men And Volts.* New York, 1941.

Henderson, Archibald. *Contemporary Immortals.* New York, 1930.

Howe, Henry. *Historical Collections Of Ohio.* Vol. I. Norwalk, O., 1896.

Howell, John W. and Schroeder, Henry. *History of the Incandescent Light.* Schenectady, N. Y., 1927.

Hoyt Jr., Edwin P. *The House of Morgan.* New York, 1966.

Hubbard, Elbert. *Little Journeys.* Vol. I. New York, 1916.

Iles. George. *Flame, Electricity and the Camera.* New York, 1900.

.................................... *Inventors at Work.* New York, 1906.

Jehl, Francis. *Menlo Park Reminiscences.* 3 vols. Dearborn, 1936.

Jenkins, Warren. *Ohio Gazeteer & Travelers Guide.* Columbus, 1837.

Jenks, William L. *St. Clair County; Its History And Its People.* Vol. I. Chicago, 1912.

Johnson, Robert U. *Remembered Yesterdays.* Boston, 1923.

Jones, Francis A. *Thomas Alva Edison.* New York, 1908.

.................................... *Thomas Alva Edison; An Intimate Record.* New York, 1924.

Josephson, Matthew. *Edison: A Biography.* New York, 1959.

Law, Frederick H. *Modern Great Americans.* New York, 1926.

Lesley, R. W. *History of the Portland Cement Industry.* Chicago, 1924.

Leupp, Francis E. *George Westinghouse.* Boston, 1919.

Lewis, Floyd E. *The Incandescent Light.* New York, 1961.

Lief, Alfred. *Harvey Firestone.* New York, 1951.

Logan, Herschel C. *Buckskin and Satin.* Harrisburg, Pa., 1955.

Marden, Orison S. *How They Succeeded.* Boston, 1901.

Marshall, David T. *Recollections of Edison.* Boston, 1931.

.................................... *Forty Years of Edison Service; 1881-1922.* New York, 1922.

McClure, J. B. *Edison And His Inventions.* Chicago, 1879.

Meadowcroft, William H. *The Boy's Life Of Edison.* New York, 1911.

Miller, Francis T. *Thomas A. Edison; Benefactor Of Mankind.* Chicago, 1931.

Nerney, Mary C. *Thomas A. Edison; A Modern Olympian.* New York, 1934.

Prescott, George B. *The Speaking Telephone.* New York, 1879.

Probst, George E. (editor) *The Indispensible Man.* New York, 1962.

Read, Oliver and Welch, Walter L. *From Tin Foil To Stereo.* Indianapolis, 1959.

Runes, Dagobert D. (editor) *The Diary And Sundry Observations Of Thomas Alva Edison.* New York, 1948.

Russell, Laurence J. *Tour Notes of the Edison Birthplace.* Milan, O., 1968.

Ryan, James A. *The Town Of Milan.* Sandusky, O., 1928.

Silverberg, Robert. *Light for the World; Edison and the Power Industry.* Princeton, N. J., 1967.

Simonds, William A. *Edison, His Life, His Work, His Genius.* New York, 1934.

Speiden, Norman R. "Thomas A. Edison: Sketch Of Activities, 1874-1881." *Science Magazine,* Vol. 105, No. 2719 (February 7, 1947).

Spring, Agnes W. "Did Edison Get 'Turned On' In Wyoming?" *True West Magazine* (June, 1968).

Stevenson, O. J. *The Talking Wire*. New York, 1947.

Stieringer, Luther. *The Life And Inventions Of Thomas A. Edison*. New York, 1890.

Stringfellow, G. E. *Edison's Contributions To Modern Transportation*. Orange, N. J., 1929.

Tate, Alfred O. *Edison's Open Door*. New York, 1938.

Taylor, A. Hoyt. "Thomas A. Edison And The Naval Research Laboratory." *Science Magazine*, Vol. 105, No. 2719 (February 7, 1947).

Thompson, Robert L. *Wiring A Continent*. Princeton, N. J., 1947.

Thorp, Raymond W. *Doc W. F. Carver; Spirit Gun of the West*. Glendale, Cal., 1957.

Verneuil, Louis. *The Fabulous Life of Sarah Bernhardt*. New York, 1942.

Villard, Henry. *Memoirs*. 2 vols. Boston, 1904.

Villard, Oswald G. *Fighting Years*. New York, 1939.

Wile, Frederic W. *Emile Berliner; Maker of the Microphone*. Indianapolis, 1926.

Wise, W. A. *Thomas A. Edison, The Youth And His Times*. Chicago, 1933.

Wheeler, Francis R. *Thomas Alva Edison*. New York, 1931.

White, Wallace B. *Milan Township and Village; One Hundred and Fifty Years*. Milan, O., 1959.

**FISH STORY.** Edison and son Charles on a cooperative venture at Ft. Myers, Florida. Ca 1900. Edison National Historic Site.

171

# INDEX

Fire of 1914 in burning out Edison's plant left this photo on which Thomas A. Edison wrote "Never touched me!"

For those who wish to visit or contact places associated with the Edison story the following list may be consulted:

Thomas Edison Birthplace Museum
9 Edison Drive
Milan, Ohio 44846

Greenfield Village
Oakwood Boulevard
Dearborn, Michigan 48121

American Film Institute
J.F.K. Center for the Performing Arts
Washington, D. C.  20036

Edison National Historic Site
Main Street and Lakeside Avenue
West Orange, New Jersey 07052

Tower of Light
Christie Street
Menlo Park, New Jersey 08871

Port Huron Museum of Arts and History
1115 Sixth Street
Port Huron, Michigan 48060

Schenectady Co. Historical Museum
32 Washington Avenue
Schenectady, New York 12305

Mount Vernon Museum of Incandescent
Lighting
717 Washington Place
Baltimore, Maryland 21202

Edison Home Museum
2350 McGregor Boulevard
Fort Myers, Florida 33901

Thomas Edison's Butchertown House
729 East Washington Street
Louisville, Kentucky 40202

Edison's first electric locomotive at Menlo Park in 1880 was the beginning.; more than a century later, many of the world's railways were still not electrified. The first mass-produced electric locomotive shown here was the Pennsylvania Railroad DD-1, developed in 1909 for the Pennsylvania Station and Tunnel complex to Manhattan.

Photo F. R. Dirkes, Ron Ziel Collection.